MORE 'REVEREND SIRS, LADIES AND GENTLEMEN . . .'

'MUMMY SAYS, WHATEVER YOU'RE SELLING, SHE DOESN'T WANT ANY . . .'

More 'Reverend Sirs, Ladies and Gentlemen . . .'

Compiled by
Don Lewis

FOREWORD BY GEOFFREY WHEELER

ILLUSTRATIONS BY BILL BOWDEN

Irreverent parables and light-hearted anecdotes dug out of dusty biographies, culled from sources both ancient and modern, purloined and exchanged in the company of clergy and laity in the firm belief that laughter and humour are elements in the nature of God himself.

MOWBRAYS
LONDON & OXFORD

Printed in Great Britain at
The Pitman Press, Bath

ISBN 0 264 64615 0

First published in 1973

For

Jonathan Vickery
Jonathan Williams
Jonathan Moss
Julian Howells

My Godsons
God help them

ACKNOWLEDGEMENTS

A collection of this nature necessarily owes much to the work of others, and the compiler is prodigiously obliged to many, both living and dead, known and unknown, named and un-named in this book. But in particular, he has to record his thanks to the Lord Bishop of London, the Lord Bishop of Liverpool, Archdeacon L. G. Fisher, Archdeacon F. H. House, OBE, Canons J. Hunter and W. G. Hurlow, Father Aidan, SSF, the Reverends E. C. Grey, J. Heywood, G. W. N. Archer, R. S. Moore, A. L. M. Davies, the Rural Dean and members of the Bowden Deanery Chapter; also to Sir Leslie Roberts, Gordon Wilcox and members of Hale Golf Club; to David Maclean, to Captain Clark, CA and J. Pearce; to Rowland Dale, and Joe Walton of Altrincham Crematorium; to J. G. Ashton, A. Gresty and W. Borrows, funeral directors; to Mrs Jones; also to the organist, Duncan Eyre, Valentine Elliot and John Boulton for 'The Conversion of the Ethiopian Eunuch', and to Geoffrey Wheeler for his stories as well as his foreword.

The compiler's thanks, too, are recorded to the *Church Times* for copyright sanction; to Miss Dorothy Collins, and Methuen & Co. for permission to include 'A Broadminded Bishop Rebukes the Verminous St Francis' by G. K. Chesterton taken from *The Collected Poems of G. K. Chesterton*; and to Mrs Williams, FLA and her staff at Hale Library.

Every effort has been made to trace the owners of copyright. If through inadvertence any rights still surviving have not been acknowledged, the compiler craves pardon of the owners.

Last and lastingly, thanks go to Ann Lewis, the compiler's wife and ghost.

CONTENTS

You're at an evening party, with
A group of pleasant folks—
You venture quietly to crack
The least of little jokes—
A lady doesn't catch the point,
And begs you to explain—
Alas for one that drops a jest
And takes it up again!

You're talking deep philosophy
With very special force,
To edify a clergyman
With suitable discourse—
You think you've got him—when he calls
A friend across the way,
And begs you'll say that funny thing
You said the other day!

You drop a pretty jeu-de-mot
Into a neighbour's ears,
Who likes to give you credit for
The clever thing he hears,
And so he hawks your jest about,
The old authentic one,
Just breaking off the point of it,
And leaving out the pun!

JOHN G. SAXE
from Comic Miseries.

FOREWORD
by Geoffrey Wheeler

At St Peter's Church, Hale it was the morning of the live television outside broadcast.

The congregation, assembled an hour and a half before the usual time, had already given a promising rehearsal and all was going well. Suddenly just before transmission, a generator failed, plunging the church into semi-darkness.

The programme opened with an outside shot of the Church as the choir processed to the south door. Pausing, the Vicar turned to deliver his opening piece to the camera. He bade the viewers welcome, then:

'This is our monthly Family Service' he said, 'It is very informal—anything goes. And something already has—the lighting . . .'

The Vicar was, and, at the time of writing, still is, Don Lewis. As one of his readers in both the literal as well as the ecclesiastical sense of the term, I warmly welcome this, the third of his anthologies.

Knowing Don is a stimulating experience, but when people know that you know him it can be a hazard—if you are in a hurry, that is. They all want to tell you stories to tell him.

Why is it that stories about the clergy should b particularly funny? A member asked comedian Ken Dodd that very question and added 'I would have thought that you would have found us rather dull and stodgy'.

'Don't you believe it,' said Ken, 'You clergymen are a Godsend to us.'

Here they are once more then, that welcome band of brothers, from the absent-minded bishop to the tactful curate.

'——THEY'LL GO WELL WITH THE USUAL TRIPE WE GET FROM THE VISITING PREACHER . . .'

1
ADAM'S RIB

The female sex is more resolute in all evil than the male (*Giraldus Cambrensis*)

Adam alone could not be easy,
So he must have a wife, an't please ye:
And how did he procure his wife
To cheer his solitary life?
Why, from a rib cut off his side
Was form'd this necessary bride.
But how did he the pain beguile?
Pho! he slept sweetly all the while.
But when this rib was re-applied,
In woman's form, to Adam's side,
How then, I pray you, did it answer?
He never slept so sweet again, Sir!

Forbidden fruit

A bishop was seated at dinner next to his hostess, a charming lady of rare beauty, but was surprised and somewhat nonplussed at not being offered anything to drink either before or during the meal, while the other guests and the lady herself, partook liberally. Finally, 'spitting feathers', he said,

'Do you think I could have a glass of wine?'

Throwing up her hands in horror his hostess answered, 'Bishop! I'm so sorry. I thought you were Chairman of the Temperance Society.'

'No,' said he, as kindly as possible, 'in actual fact I am Chairman of the Anti-vice Campaign.'

'Ah!' she replied, 'I knew there was something I couldn't offer you.'

Appleless Adam

A speaker on women's suffrage once challenged her audience with the rhetorical question, 'Where, I ask you, where would man be today if it were not for woman?' A deep voice from the back of the hall answered: 'In the Garden of Eden eating strawberries.'

The curse of Eve and the wiles of Adam

When Eve would try, but to her cost,
  Th' experiment of evil,
That she with gods might wisdom boast,
  And cunning with the devil.
Too soon the knowledge she obtain'd;
  Too late she cursed the prize;
Oh! had she but a fool remain'd,
  We should have all been wise.

'You called, Madam?'

A little girl came home from Sunday School and told her mother: 'I heard such a lovely story about a man called Adam and a woman called Eve, who were so happy until the servant came.'

Bull-rush confusion

A Sunday School teacher said to one of her children: 'King Pharoah's daughter found the baby Moses, in the bull-rushes, didn't she?'

'So she said, Miss,' was the reply.

Holiday - Old Testament style

'What,' said the Sunday School teacher to the class, 'do you know about Elijah?'

'Not very much is known of this holy man,' replied one of the scholars, 'but we do know that he went on a cruise with a widow.'

Qualified kindness to questionable kinsmen

A vagrant came to the Rectory door and asked for help from the parson's wife using the plea that they were of the same family.

'How can that possibly be, my man?' asked the Rector's wife.

'Well surely, ma'am, we're both descended from Adam?' he said, hoping he would not be refused.

'Here is a penny for you,' said she, 'and if all the rest of your relations give you as much you will be much richer than we are.'

Little strokes fell great oaks

A professor of Divinity was once asked by a student for a brief, short rule of life. He offered the following:

'Fear no man and do right. Fear all women—and do not write.'

An empty command

A bachelor dignitary of the Church had been partaking rather liberally of the juice of the grape at a conference. When he was taken up to his hotel room, or rather, the room which the porter thought was his, they found, carefully laid out on the bed, a dainty, lacy, naughty night-dress. The Church dignitary surveyed this solemnly, and finally, in shrewd tones, he asked,

'What's this?'

'Well, that,' replied the porter who did not know whether the gentleman expected a lady or not, 'that is a ladies' night-dress.'

The dignitary touched it, sniffed the delicate perfume, turned to the porter and commanded, in his best ecclesiastical voice,

'Take it away, and fill it.'

Cost of discipleship

When the first experiment in team ministry was tried in Manchester one young curate connected with the team did a tremendous amount of work at night-time around the various clubs, amongst strippers and entertainers. The well-meaning curate used to make enquiries about the conditions under which some of the part-time girls worked. He discovered that one girl only earned five pounds a week so he said to her,

'It is surely almost impossible to lead a good Christian life on such a small wage?'

'On the contrary,' replied the young lady, 'it is the only kind of life you can lead on five pounds a week!'

Crock calling the kettle

A preacher who was in the habit of mumbling his words when preaching his sermon dropped in for tea, one afternoon, with a somewhat sour lady of his congregation.

As she poured him a cup of tea, he noticed that the pot wasn't pouring properly.

'I'm afraid Mrs Jones' he said, 'that your teapot isn't doing its job very well.'

'No indeed,' came Mrs Jones' reply, 'its like yourself Vicar, it has a very poor delivery'.

Curate's parting shot

A curate was just leaving the parish to take up an incumbency when he was presented with a silver tea service. Rising to thank the members of the congregation he said, 'I will not call you ladies and gentlemen for I know you too well for that.'

And thy clouds drop fatness (*Psalm* 65, 12)

It is amazing what some people pick up from sermons. One dear lady who was weight-conscious came to her vicar and complained that in his sermon he had said that 'constant dripping would wear away a stone.'

'Well, it does,' replied the vicar.

'But,' said the lady with indignation, 'I've eaten it with every meal since hearing your sermon and instead of losing a stone, I've put one on.'

Mon chou

When Dr Whately was Rector of Halesworth he chanced to remark to a lady about a mutual acquaintance that she was 'an old cabbage'. When this reached the ears of the lady she was grossly offended and took the Rector to task in no uncertain manner and asked him what he meant by calling her an old cabbage.

'So you are, my dear madam,'—said Dr Whately, —'all heart.'

Thirteen summers and a few winters

Lady Wallace was speaking to David Hume, the historian, on one occasion;

'Pray, Sir, as I am often asked what age I am, what answer should I make?'

Mr Hume immediately guessing her ladyship's meaning said, 'Madam, when you are asked that question again answer that you are not yet come to the years of discretion.'

**'As women in speech can revile a man,
So can they in silence beguile a man' (*Tarlton*)**

At a meeting of the Mothers' Union recently the vicar was one of four speakers on a panel, the other three being women;

'Would you mind having the last word Vicar?' said the lady chairman sweetly.

'By no means,' was the reply, 'I should rather enjoy it being a married man.'

Painted Puritans

Even during the Puritan rule after the death of Charles I, it would appear that cosmetics were still used.

'Our English ladies, who seemed to have borrowed some of their cosmetical conceits from barbarous nations, are seldom known to be contented with a face of God's making; for they are either adding, detracting, or altering continually, having many facusses in readiness for the same purpose. Sometimes they think they have too much colour, then they use art to make them look pale and fair; now they have too little colour, then Spanish paper, red leather, or other cosmetical rubricks, must be had. Yet, for all this, it may be, the skins of their faces do not please them, off they go with mercury water, and so they remain, like peeled ewes, until their faces have recovered a new epidermis. Our ladies have lately entertained a vain custom of spotting their faces, out of an effectation of a mole to set off their beauty, such as Venus had, and it is well if one black patch will serve to make their faces remarkable; for some fill their visages full of them, varied into all manner of shapes and figures.'

Anthropometamorphosis John Bulwer 1650

False pretences

'That all women, of whatever age, rank, profession, or degree, whether virgins, maids, or widows, that shall, from and after such Act, impose upon, seduce, and betray into matrimony, any of His Majesty's subjects, by the scent, paints, cosmetic washes, artificial teeth, false hair, Spanish wool, iron stays, hoops, high-heeled shoes, bolstered hips, shall incur the penalty of the law now in force against witchcraft and like misdemeanours, and that the marriage, upon conviction, shall stand null and void.'

(Act of Parliament 1770)

Heat resistant

The Reverend Dr Brown had paid his attention to a certain lady for a great many years but with no success. During that time it had been his custom to drink her health on every conceivable occasion. One evening he omitted the ceremony.

'Come, Dr Brown,' said his friend, 'drink your toast to your lady.'

The doctor replied, 'I have toasted her for many years and I find that I cannot make her Brown so I'll not toast her any longer.'

'A woman is a book, and often found
To prove far better in the sheets, than bound;
No wonder then, some students take delight,
Above all things, to study in the night.'

... I begin to hate these dapper young-ladies' preachers like the devil, for I am sickened and enraged to see silly women blown about with every wind, falling in love with the preacher instead of his sermon, and with his sermon instead of the Bible.

Charles Kingsley when a student.

Go man, go

A curate who was a ladies' man had become very popular in the parish and his vicar had no alternative but to ask him to find another place of work.

'Oh it's all right, Vicar,' said the young man, 'there's safety in numbers.'

'That's where you're wrong,' replied the older and wiser cleric, 'your only safety is in Exodus.'

Sexless society

There was a young fellow called Adam.
Long hair and tight jeans, yes he had 'em.
He started to bristle,
When he got an epistle
Which began 'Dear Sir and/or Madam ...'

Conditioned to the bottle

It has been suggested that young men admire the small cone-shaped breast in women rather than the fuller drooping breast because it reminds them of the feeding-bottle. George IV once discussed this theory with Sheridan who, with a twinkle, replied, 'No poet, sir, has ever written in praise of a feeding-bottle.'

Talent exposure

Thrown from her steed, a lovely maid,
Unconscious what her fall had betray'd,
With nimble leap her seat regain'd,
While motionless her chaplain remain'd:
'Why, sir, you seem surpris'd!' said she,
'At seeing my agility.'
'Mayhap,' quoth he, 'that word from London
came,
But here we give it quite a different name.'

The love tithe

A clergyman once replied to a young lady who had sent him her compliments on a playing card, the ten of hearts:

'Your compliments, Lady, I pray you
forbear,
Our old English service is much more
sincere;
You sent me ten hearts; the tithe's only
mine;
Give me but your own, you may burn
t'other nine.'

A Divine marries a Churchman!

Richard Hooker in 1581 was appointed to preach at St Paul's Cross, and met his 'fate' in the process. The events surrounding this preaching engagement led to his marriage. Hooker rode from Oxford to London and was given hospitality in the home of a Mr and Mrs Churchman. When he arrived he was ill and Mrs Churchman provided him with medicine and a warm bed and he recovered sufficiently to preach. The good lady persuaded him that a wife to nurse him would be the answer to his somewhat delicate health and Hooker allowed Mrs Churchman to select a wife for him. A year later when he returned to preach in London she married him to her daughter Joan, not a beauty but Hooker was short-sighted and had little knowledge of the ways of the other sex.

'She proved,' said Walton, 'to be the sort of wife whom Solomon compared to "a dripping house", so that thenceforth he was constrained to "dwell with Meshech, and have his habitation among the tents of Kedar". It was an unwise marriage where his only comfort was in the thought that "affliction is a Divine diet".'

Grim fairy tale

She was reading a book which had been a present for her eighth birthday when she suddenly blurted out,

'Mummy, do fairy tales always begin with "Once upon a time"?'

'Not always my darling,' said Mother, glancing at the clock, 'quite often they begin with, "I have been unavoidably detained at the office".'

Sublime sublimation

The spinster laughed at anyone who suggested that it was hard luck she had not managed to get a husband.

'I have a dog that growls, a parrot that swears, a goat that has a good beard, a fireplace that smokes, and a cat that stays out all night. Why should I want a husband?'

Carry on Vicar

It was a Welsh vicar of a country town in Montgomeryshire who announced in church one Sunday that he was desperately short of Sunday school teachers. 'Ideally,' he said, 'I would like three or four ladies to come and help. At present I am forced to carry on with two ladies from an adjoining parish.'

Happiness is heart shaped

A somewhat raw young curate was putting up a special prayer for the young men among his worshippers; it was no surprise that a hearty 'Amen' came from all that quarter of the congregation, when he prayed:

'Lord give them all pure hearts, give them all clean hearts, give them all sweet hearts.'

'I JUST KNEW IT COULDN'T LAST . . .!'

2
HOLY DEADLOCK

Hard luck folks

Bishop J. C. Jones of Bangor when preaching at a marriage service at Caernarvon parish church, turned to the newly married bride and groom and said, 'You came to this church today to get the blessing of God on your union. Well you've had it!'

Pillion pal

At most weddings it is the custom for the officiating clergyman to give a short sermon to the bride and bridegroom on their duties to each other in the marriage state. On one occasion the clergyman said to the bride, 'It is your privilege and duty to follow your husband wherever he may go, being at his side to help him in all adversity.'

The bride chipped in, 'Well that's going to be tough on me, sir, isn't it? My husband is a speedway rider.'

Inanimate couple

In a certain church it was the practice for the parson to keep the banns book on the righthand side of his reading desk. He had begun to announce the banns as usual, 'I publish the banns of marriage . . .' while reaching out his hand to take the book, but on this occasion it was not there.

In order to gain time he started again, 'I publish the banns of marriage . . .' but he still could not find the missing book.

Just then the verger came to him and in a stage whisper that could be heard all over the church announced, 'Between the cushion and desk, sir.'

Reverend worldly goods

A young curate was being married and the whole congregation in the church heard his lovely and perhaps deliberate spoonerism. The vicar who was officiating said,

'Repeat after me, "with all my worldly goods I thee endow".'

'With all my *goodly words* I thee endow,' came the rejoinder.

Count corrected

A former curate of Stoke being very anxious to do things rubrically, insisted on the ring being put on the 'fourth finger' at a wedding he took. The woman resisted and said, 'I would sooner die than be married on my little finger.'

The curate said, 'But the rubric says so.'

Thereupon the verger stepped forward and saved the day, 'In these cases, sir, the thoomb counts as a digit.'

Wise before the fall

In these days when bridegroom, best man, groomsman, and even guests are dressed somewhat alike, it is always difficult for the verger or parson to determine the principal. The clergyman tried to pick out the bridegroom by choosing the man with the biggest buttonhole.

He asked him quietly, 'Are you the happy man?'

'That remains to be seen,' came the reply from the young fellow.

'But,' said the clergyman, 'are you the man who is to be married?'

'Oh yes,' came the reply, 'but that's another matter.'

Rough reception

A clergyman wanted to send a greetings telegram to a girl from his parish who was being married whilst he was on holiday. He put in the telegram a Biblical reference: 1 John 4. 18 ('There is no fear in love, but perfect love casteth out fear'). Nothing could be nicer; but the Post Office clerk writing out the telegram omitted the initial figure, changing the reference to the Gospel of St John.

The best man during the reception read out the text from the Bible, and reduced the bride to tears, for the words he spoke were, 'He whom thou hast is not thy husband.'

Fee reduction on compassionate grounds

Old John presented himself at the Vicarage to put in his banns to be married for the third time.

'I'm an old customer, Vicar, so I hope ye'll do the job cheap. Strike off two thirds of the fee as it's the third wife.'

'I know not which live more unnatural lives, Obeying husbands or commanding wives.'

(*Francis Quarles*)

The curate of St John's Church, Wrexham, in 1959 was of Welsh origin and certainly had the gift of oratory. His main weakness in the pulpit lay in the fact that people got so completely immersed in his sermons that they tended to think aloud.

'The man who gives in when he is wrong,' he said on one occasion, 'is a wise and prudent man; but the man who gives in when he is right is . . .'

'Married,' interjected a hen-pecked voice in the congregation.

Self-inflicted punishment

A parishioner came to his vicar to complain that his third wife was giving him a very rough time, and wanted the vicar to do something about it. He told the vicar that his first wife, 'was a very good wife but the Lord took her.' His second wife was 'bad and the devil took her.'

'Now I've got one who's ten times worse and I can't get anyone to take her.'

Crossword clue

Dean Swift when visiting an inn called The Three Crosses found the landlady's manner not to his liking, so before he left he wrote on the window with his diamond:

To the Landlord.
There hang three crosses at thy door
Hang up thy wife and she'll make four.

Ideal group practice

Dr George Reindorp, Bishop of Guildford, on his marriage:

'My wife is a medical doctor, and I'm a doctor of divinity. So you might call ours a marriage of body and soul.'

Reception *faux-pas*

Mr Grindrod, introduced by Mr Swinburne as his successor, began by saying;

'I hope I shall not make any *faux-pas* today, like that of the nervous bridegroom who, when called upon for a speech, stretching out his hand in the direction of his bride at his side began—"I do not know why this thing is thrust upon me".'

One wife too many

'Just look at that headline in this morning's paper,' said the vicar's wife, who had been making the marriage somewhat a trial for her husband. ' "One wife too many." It must be another of those sordid accounts about a bigamist!'

The vicar not daring so much as to raise his eyes from his cornflakes said in a mild voice, 'Not necessarily, my darling.'

Up-dated parable

It would appear that not all clergymen share matrimonial bliss. One Sunday morning a parson was preaching on the parable of the Great Supper—'and another said, "I have bought five yoke of oxen, and I go to prove them, I pray thee have me excused. And another said, "I have married a wife, and therefore I cannot come". ' There was a long pause, the parson took a deep breath and said philosophically, 'the fact is my dear friends, one woman can draw a man further away from the Kingdom of Heaven than fifty yoke of oxen.'

'Man has his will—but woman has her way.'

(*O. W.Holmes*)

A vicar had received an offer of a very good living and one of his churchwardens called at the Vicarage to find out whether or not he was going to move to the new parish. The maid answered the door.

'You can't see him,' she said, 'the vicar is in his study praying, seeking guidance from God as to whether he should move to the new parish or not.'

'Then can I see the vicar's wife ?' asked the churchwarden.

'I'm afraid not, sir, you see she's upstairs, packing.'

Delicate regal insult

Sir John Harrington in his *Nugae Antiquae* records that Queen Elizabeth I, who did not approve of clergy marriage, visited Archbishop Parker and his lady. On leaving she expressed her thanks to the Archbishop, and then the Queen turned to his wife and said, 'And you, *madam* I may not call you, and *mistress* I am ashamed to call you, but yet I do thank you.'

'Woman is a creature without reason, who pokes the fire from the top' (*Archbishop Whately*)

It was Archbishop Whately who told of his wife's visit to a haberdasher's shop. She asked for some articles she had purchased to be sent to her home. The draper, not knowing her, was rather reluctant to render this service.

'Sir,' said Mrs Whately, with offended dignity, 'I am the Archbishop's lady.'

'I don't care if you are his wife,' replied the shop-keeper.

Hubby hobby

An old country clerk in showing visitors round the churchyard used to stop at a certain tombstone and say;

'This 'ere is the tomb of Thomas 'Ooper and 'is eleven wives.' One day a lady remarked, 'Eleven? Dear me, that's rather a lot, isn't it?' The old man looked at her gravely and replied, 'Well, mum, yer see it was an' 'obby of 'is'n.'

Matrimonial tears

On his death-bed poor Lubin lies;
His spouse is in despair;
With frequent sobs, and mutual cries,
They both express their care.

A diff'rent cause, says parson Sly,
The same effect may give
Poor Lubin fears that he shall die;
His wife, that he may live.

(Matthew Prior 1664–1721)

Evolved, or Created?

A curate, in the days when the Darwinian theories were startling men's minds, once said to Bishop Wilberforce, 'I don't see that it would have made any difference to me if my great-great-grandfather had been an ape.'

'No,' replied the Bishop, 'perhaps not; but it would have made some difference to your great-great-grandmother.'

Scriptural match making

A teacher on one occasion was giving a lesson on the New Testament.

'Can anyone tell me what is an epistle?'

'Please Miss, an epistle is the wife of an Apostle.'

P.S.

A clergyman once announced during the notices, 'On Friday, the ladies of the Mothers' Union will hold a rummage sale. This is a chance for all the ladies of the congregation to get rid of anything that is not worth keeping but is too good to be thrown away. Don't forget to bring your husbands.'

'I verily believe that very few clergyman will be saved.' (*St John Chrysostom*)

A divine was once asked by one of his lady acquaintances why there were no marriages in heaven. With a twinkle in his eye, the divine replied, 'Well for the simple reason, that there are no ladies there.'

'Nonsense! Quite the contrary,' came the reply, 'there are women in heaven all right; the trouble is they cannot find the priests to marry them.'

'I WONDER IF YOU COULD DIRECT ME TO THE CREMATORIUM . . .?'

3
LATE LAMENTED

Occasional words for Occasional offices

A vicar who used to preach verbatim from his sermon notes was asked to preach the sermon at a funeral. He had to rush to the church, and hurriedly picked up the first manuscript on his desk. He was shattered when he found after mounting the pulpit, that he had extracted from his sermon stock the one which began with the text, 'And the beggar died'.

Well, well, well

At one time funeral sermons were common in England and it is recorded that the last place where the custom lingered was the Island of Portland, in Dorsetshire. For preaching such a sermon the preacher received a fee of half a guinea. When the infamous Madam Cresswell died she made provision in her will for her funeral sermon to be preached but the payment of the fee was conditional upon the clergyman speaking 'well' of her. This was a difficult task in view of her career, but the clergyman who undertook the sermon spent sometime preaching on death without any reference to the deceased lady. He then concluded with the following:

'By the will of the deceased it is expected that I should mention her and say nothing but what was well of her. All that I shall therefore say of her is this: she was born well, lived well, and died well, for she was born with the name of Cresswell, she lived in Clerkenwell and she died in Bridewell.'

A saving farewell

The barber at Welshpool had had a busy time: it was market day and in between buying and selling stock, the local farmers had been pouring into his shop to have his professional attention to themselves, but just before he pulled down the blind, a breathless youth rushed into say that Mrs Jenkins was sending for him urgently as her husband had just died.

'Old Will passed away!' exclaimed the barber in sad astonishment, 'he was a good customer of mine. I'll get my coat and come with you at once.'

At the house he knocked and was admitted by the widow, a tart old woman whose indifference to her husband's death was callously obvious.

'I see you got the message,' she said. 'Will Jenkins died this morning and I've called you over to give him a shave. How much will it cost?' she rapped in the same breath. The barber paused. Old Will had been pretty good by and large; and he'd not charge his widow the full fee.

'Sixpence,' he replied.

'Sixpence,' was the incredulous retort, 'that's far too much. No thank you, sir, I'll not put you to the trouble.' And then, as she opened the door for him, 'Far too much, sixpence, he can do without a shave. See, it's not as if he was going anywhere special.'

A tolling text

A country parson took his text from St Mark I. 30: 'Now Simon's mother-in-law lay sick with a fever.' He preached for three successive Sundays on the same subject. Soon after the last occasion when he used the text, two of the congregation were going home across the churchyard, and, hearing the church bell toll one of them asked the other who it was for.

'I can't rightly say unless it is for Peter's wife's mother for she has been sick of a fever these last three weeks.'

Disappointing diet

Sir Patrick Hume died in 1714 aged eighty-four. Lord Binning visiting him when he was on his death-bed observed the old man smiling so he asked him what he was amused by.

Sir Patrick answered, 'I am diverted to think what a disappointment the worms will meet with when they bore through my coffin expecting to get a good meal, and get nothing but bones.'

It is time to bumpy

The Reverend R. S. Hawker, Vicar of Morwenstow, used to tell the following story concerning one of his predecessors.

A certain deformed person living in that area had become a jester. That is, he was on the butt end of most of the local jokes. As Black John grew older he took to wandering about gypsy fashion and while he found a welcome at most cottages and farm houses, his usual bed was among the reeds or ferns. One day in a snow storm he was missed and a search was made for him. They found him in the snow, cold and stiff and, to all appearance, dead. He was carried home, placed in a coffin and carried towards the graveyard.

Just as the clergyman who was reading the Service came to the words which committed the body to the ground, a loud thumping noise was heard inside the coffin. The bystanders opened the lid quickly and up sat Black John, alive. He had been restored to life by the motion and warmth of his funeral ride.

As he told the astonished mourners, he heard the words 'dust to dust' and then, he said, 'I thought it was high time to bumpy.' This phrase became a Cornish proverb in due course: 'It is time to bumpy as Black John said.'

His sudden resurrection, however, turned his mind somewhat and more than once the reverend gentleman who took his funeral service to no avail was suddenly assaulted in his preambulations around the parish, by a stone hurled at him from a hedge, followed by an angry cry, in a well-known voice, of 'Aha! Old Dust-to-Dust! Here I be, alive and kicking.'

Say it with flowers

The committee responsible for building a crematorium stood in trepidation of criticism from the community in which it was erected. Much to their surprise, however, not a single voice of censure was raised. But after the new crematorium was finally completed the superintendent received a letter from an old lady who, after congratulating him on the masterly design of the building and saying what a valuable contribution it would be to the community, went on: 'But tell me, please, whose idea it was to plant out the two flower beds flanking the entrance to the crematorium with red-hot-pokers?'

Miserly memento

A Manchester undertaker tells the story of a doctor who died who had been, in his lifetime, the meanest of men. He left a stipulation in his will, that his funeral arrangements should be as cheap as possible.

The day for the interment arrived. The funeral director brought the corpse to the cemetery in a coffin made of the cheapest wood obtainable.

When the service was over, the vicar, who knew of the doctor's request to have everything done as cheaply as possible, looked down into the grave and noticed that on the coffin was a brass plate, beautifully engraved, but he could not read what it said.

Returning to the undertaker he asked, 'Why is it that when Dr Murphy wanted everything done so cheaply, you put an expensive brass plate on the coffin lid?'

The funeral director turning to him, said, 'Well if you look carefully, Vicar, you will see that it reads:

"Harold Murphy, M.D.
Surgery hours: 9–10.30 am
5.30–6.30 pm".'

Free will at last

Willie dying intestate, his relatives claim'd,
Whilst his widow most vilely his memory defamed.
'What,' cries she, 'must I suffer because the old knave,
Without leaving a will, is laid snug in his grave?'
'That's no wonder,' says one, 'for 'tis very well known,
Since he married, poor man, he'd no will of his own.'

On spec!

It was in Castleton that the story of the lady who was once caretaker of the parish church at Kirby Lonsdale was told; she was never short of an answer. The village lawyer was going through the church-yard one day when the bell was tolling and, meeting the lady-verger, asked,

'Hello my dear, whose funeral is it this time?'

'Oh! it's no-one but Mrs So and So.'

Not having had any news of her decease, he replied, 'I did not know she was dead.'

The lady-verger's answer reflects some of the strange beliefs at that time.

'Well, what with these new fangled trances and spiritual-like hokey pokey, I don't know myself for a certainty but at least the sexton has dug her grave and the funeral's booked in so we must bury her on speculation.'

Better the cough than the coffin

On his way through the graveyard to church, Ben Jenkins, Vicar of Penymaes heard the most lung-rending cough coming from his left. Inspection did not immediately yield its source, so he digressed from his errand to have a closer look. Suddenly, (and almost literally), he came upon Tobias his old grave digger: five and a half foot down in the grave he was working on, and almost in a state of collapse from the paroxism.

'Tobias! You take care, Tobias! That's a very severe cough you have,' counselled the priest solicitously. The other glared back at him and snorted, 'Huh! There's many a one lying around me here who'd be glad of a cough like that.'

Bundled out head and heels

Sir Walter Scott's remark at the funeral ceremony of the eccentric Earl of Buchan, deserves mention. In accordance with the Christian tradition, the body should have been carried into the chapel where it was to be interred, feet first. Sir David Brewster was one of the mourners and observed that the head of the coffin went in first. He said, 'We have brought the Earl's head in the wrong way.'

'Never mind,' replied Scott, 'his lordship's head was turned when he was alive, and it is not worth our while to shift it now.'

On a doctor turned undertaker

Celsus, who late, though void of skill,
  Profess'd the healing art,
Now acts, in league with Pluto still,
  The undertaker's part.
The Doctor's practice tending more
  To slaughter than to save,
Is now the same as 'twas before,
  To send folks to their grave.

A helping hand

It was after what the undertaker called a 'Warrington works funeral' that the widow of the firm's director was profuse in her thanks to the bearers: putting her hand on the youngest bearer's shoulder she said, 'Thank you so very, very much.'

'Think nothing of it,' said the lad, 'it was a pleasure.'

Buried error

Peter Priestly, parish clerk and grave digger of Wakefield in the middle of the eighteenth century was a great character. On one occasion he was lettering a gravestone when the local physician came by. Looking at his handiwork the doctor remarked, 'Why Peter, you've spelt it wrong.'

'Have I, Doctor?' said he sharply. 'Then how should it be?' When he was told how to correct his error he looked slyly into the physician's eyes and said, 'Well, well, pass it over Doctor—pass it over. I've covered up many a blot of yours.'

Is your journey really necessary?

The old Superintendent of Wrexham Cemetery in the nineteen fifties was a great wit. There was the funeral where the chief mourner was a very old man who coughed all through the committal. As he was led to the car from the graveside the superintendent took the old man by the arm and whispered, 'Do you think it's worth your while going home?'

Regimental regret

Military salutes at funerals have a special meaning. The three volleys over the grave are symbolic of the Trinity. It was also at one time believed that by firing into the air they were firing at the Devil which might get into men's minds at such moments as the burial of a comrade. The reversal of arms is an acknowledgement of the shame of killing. A sergeant-major on one occasion was putting the firing party through funeral drill and was not happy with their performance. Finally, he had an idea and said to his men, 'Let's make it a little more realistic men; I'll be the corpse.'

Once more he gave them the orders and marched in between the two ranks and lay down on the ground. Looking up at them he said, 'Yes, your heads is right and your hands is right and your weapons is right but you ain't got that look of regret that you ought to have.'

Less turn you grave the parson's cattle rage,
For both his cow and horse the churchyard graze

(*Grey: 'Shepherds Week'*)

Until the year 1856, the churchyard of Chipping Norton was let to a butcher for grazing sheep. An old lady writing to a Mr Charles Holmes, of Ilfracombe, said that she 'never purchased meat from that butcher, as she thought that the sheep grazing in the churchyard gave mutton such a deathly taste.'

Crop rotation

There was once a rector who sowed part of his churchyard with turnips. A conscientious archdeacon objected and said he hoped he might not see turnips again when he came in the following year to inspect the church.

'Certainly not,' came the rector's reply, 'it'll be barley next year.'

Poetic licence

An old parish clerk was showing a group of visitors round his ancient parish church and was tending to stretch things a little.

'This,' he said to the group pointing to a skull, 'is said to be the skull of Oliver Cromwell.'

'But,' chipped in one of the visitors, 'I was shown a much larger skull than that at Oxford reputed to be Oliver Cromwell's skull."

'Ah, that may be so,' said the old verger, 'but this is his skull when he was a young man.'

Long winded

'Friend! in your epitaphs I'm grieved,
So very much is said:
One half will never be believ'd,
The other never read.'

On Dr Friend.

Frank bug-words

'Here Skugg
Lies snug,
As a bug
In a rug.'

Benjamin Franklin in a letter to his sister, Mrs Mecom, March 9, 1773.

4
FAMILY FAITH AND FAILINGS

Rev. Jack of all trades

'Wanted for a family who have bad health, a sober, steady person in the capacity of doctor, surgeon and apothecary. He must occasionally act in the capacity of butler, and dress hair and wigs. He will be required to read prayers occasionally and to preach a sermon every Sunday. The reason for this advertisement is that the family cannot any longer afford the expense of the physical tribe, and wish to be at a certain expense for their bodies and soul. A good salary will be given.'
An advertisement from the Public Advertizer, 1776

Here is talk of the Turk and the Pope, but my next neighbour doth me more harm than either of them both. (*Old Saying*)

The Reverend Mr Tweedle, a Methodist minister, who lived at Waen y Wern, Ebbw Vale, called on his next door neighbour when she had just given birth to a twelve and three quarter pound baby. Patting the cot covers, Mr Tweedle, affectionately known as Tweedle-Dum, asked,

'Well, Mrs Lewis, what's he going to be when he grows up?' Exhausted from her hard and long efforts and looking at her placid offspring careless of all but comfort, she replied,

'He's going to be like you Mr Tweedle; he's not going to work for a living."

The generation gap

'We are living in difficult and dangerous times. Youth has no regard for old age, and the wisdom of centuries is looked down upon both as stupidity and foolishness. The young men are indolent and insolent; the young women are indecent and indecorous in their speech, behaviour and dress.'

Peter the Hermit, 1114

Ugly as sin

Bishop Padget had been preaching at St Mary's, Stockport, and was returning home by train. He sat in a carriage all by himself hidden behind his newspaper. Two men got in. It so happened that they had been at the service the night before when the Bishop preached and they started discussing the sermon.

'Wonderful sermon, wasn't it?'

'Yes,' said the other, 'truly wonderful, but he must be the ugliest beggar in the world.'

Bishop Padget lowered his paper slowly, 'That statement might be true my man, but I don't think I'm as bad looking as all that. You haven't seen my brother yet.'

Two edged sword

Weary of the Vicar's dry, dusty, and lengthy sermons, one of his parishioners, at the end of her tether, made the excuse, 'If my husband goes out during the sermon Vicar, you'll have to excuse him; he's a terrible one for walking in his sleep.'

Not inattentive

Canon Ridgway, Vicar of Bowdon, was approached by a lady who appeared regularly in his Sunday morning congregation, who said to him, 'Vicar, I don't want you to think ill of me. During your sermon I always sit with my eyes tightly shut and I want to assure you, Vicar, that I am not asleep; I am in fact thinking out my shopping list for the coming week's groceries.'

Fed-up

In 1766 Robert Fergusson became a bursar at St Andrews and, as such, was entitled to his board within the College. The diet supplied by the professors was meagre and dinner usually consisted of rabbits, served with rye. It was the custom for bursars to 'say grace' in turn. When Fergusson's turn came, he prayed,

'For rabbits young and for rabbits old,
For rabbits hot and for rabbits cold,
For rabbits tender and for rabbits tough,
Our thanks we render—but we've had enough.'

Providential Aunt Sally

'Do you believe in Providential interference, My Lord?' asked a lady of Bishop Temple.

'That depends on what you mean by it,' he replied.

'Well, my aunt was suddenly prevented from going on a voyage in a ship that went down—would you call that a case of Providential interference?'

'Can't tell; didn't know your aunt.'

A lasting impression

A vicar, who held very strong views on the abolition of corporal punishment in every shape and form, was out visiting one day and called at the home of one of his sidesmen, only to find him thrashing his teenage son with his leather belt. The vicar at once began to intercede for the lad, bringing all his arguments against corporal punishment to bear. The father maintained that the lad must be trained while he was young and reinforced his argument by claiming that 'it was best to make an impression while the wax was soft.'

'True,' said the vicar, 'but that does not apply in this case since the whacks you were using were not soft.'

Look out for squalls

'In your sermon this morning vicar, you spoke of the baby you'd just baptised as a "new wave on the ocean of life",' commented the verger who had just suffered the painful noise of the new Christian's persistent howling all through the service.

'Yes,' answered the vicar, 'rather an apt poetic figure of speech I thought.'

The verger snorted, 'Fresh squall would have hit the mark better!'

Mercy on's! A barne, a very pretty barne. A boy or a child, I wonder?

(*Shakespeare: Winter's Tale, III*, 3)

There is a strange entry in the parish records of Soberton for 1585 which reads:

'John Quint half a child was crystened at home by the mydwyffe, Elizabeth Quint, the other halffe chylld was crystened at ye Churche.'

Homer sometimes nods (*old saying*)

The Rev. Studdert Kennedy used to tell the story of a baby who had been given the Christian names: Alfred Homer. When the parson who baptised the child came to filling up the Baptismal Register, he paused for a time thinking about the origin of the second name. 'Strange,' he thought, as his mind went back to the Greek poet; 'a queer name and rather out of the ordinary for a son of a working man.' Then he turned to the proud father,

'The second name of your child will be after your favourite poet I suppose?'

'Poet, sir!' said the man with a look of surprise, 'Lord no, I keeps pigeons.'

Abstinence advocated inadvertently

The Chester Diocesan President of the Mothers' Union was addressing a hall packed with young wives who had just listened to an inspiring address on Mission at their Young Wives' Festival in June 1971. With a voice which commanded attention and implied authority, she reminded them of a service scheduled for the Cathedral in March of 1972.

'Ladies,' she said, 'it is absolutely essential that you do nothing between now and March 1972 that will prevent you from coming to that very important gathering at the Cathedral.'

The visiting preacher was amused to see almost every young mother in the room running through an up-to-nine finger counting operation which was accompanied by much head shaking.

The end

It is said that a parish priest when he was baptising a child and asked the name of it, was shocked to receive the reply, 'Alpha Omega'.

'But,' he exclaimed, 'you can't give a child a name like that.'

'Oh yes, I can,' said his mother, 'and what's more, it's more than appropriate; he's the first, and,' she finished tartly, 'I hope he will be the last.'

Child of God and inheritor of the government dockyard

On the Cornish side of the estuary of the Tamar, a rector appointed at the end of the last century was turning over the register of baptisms, and was surprised at seeing the entries of the baptism of boys only.

'Why Dick,' said he to the parish clerk, 'however does this come about? Are there only boys born in this place?'

'Please your Reverence, 'tain't that, but as they won't take girls into the yard at Devonport, 'tain't no good baptising 'em.'

A baptismal certificate was necessary for admission to the Government dockyard.

A puppy dog tale

An honorary chaplain being entertained in the mess by the officers of the battalion, and not knowing much about military ceremony, was asked by one of the officers who was a bit of a wag to do him the great favour of performing the ceremony of baptism for his recently acquired boxer pup. The officers present were expecting no little merriment from the occasion. The minister replied,

'I am a minister of the Church of God and must proceed accordingly. Now Captain, I must begin with the usual question, "You acknowledge yourself the father of this puppy?"'

Bin-man-ship

A parish priest was given a meat pie by one of his parishioners. Since it was found to be almost uneatable, his wife had to throw it into the dust bin. Troubled as to how to thank the woman and be truthful at the same time, the priest eventually was able to tell her: 'I can promise you that a pie like that does not last long in our house!'

Cleanliness is next to godliness

Bishop Wilberforce was known affectionately as Soapy Sam and on one occasion he was staying with the Dean of Peterborough when the small daughter of the house went up to him and asked why he was called, Soapy Sam.

'I'm afraid I cannot tell you, my dear,' was the reply, 'unless it is that I am always in hot water but come out with clean hands.'

The cobbler's children

Having had to accept the distressing fact that his young son was passing through that obnoxious phase of bad language common to most children, the vicar was nonetheless equally painfully aware that, stemming from the vicarage, such an example would have a bad effect on the cloth, as well as being an addedly attractive temptation to his fellows.

'Simon,' he counselled solemnly, 'about this party you've been asked to: I've told Alistair's mother that the minute she hears you say anything you shouldn't, you're to be sent home.'

Duly contrite, Simon left and got ready for his party. Bidding his anxious parents 'Good bye' he set off, leaving them earnestly praying that he would not let them down again this time.

To their consternation, however, he was back in ten minutes! Their disappointment and anger knew no bounds. Soundly whacking him, they sent him up to his room and told him to stay there till morning.

An hour later though, his mother ventured upstairs and went into his room.

'Oh Simon, how could you! What did you say?'

With sullen indignation, Simon replied, 'I didn't say anything. The party's not until next week.'

Artless evangelist

Unbuttoning his coat after receiving him home from the school party, John's Mother said, 'Well John did you have a lovely time? What did you do?'

'Yes, Mum, super. We had jelly and cake and crisps, and ice cream, and sandwiches, and we played games and we had a concert and all did things like sing or play the piano or say poetry.

His Mother's face fell. John's disposition and ability to shine in the latter was well known for its absence. Hesitantly she asked, 'Er, what did you do at the concert?'

John beamed with successful pride. 'I said my prayers, Mum.'

There's a friend of dear old Grandma's

Two small children were overheard having an adult discussion about grandmother who was nearing her ninetieth birthday. She had been ill and they had caught some of the concern from their parents.

'Wouldn't it be terrible,' said one, 'if Gran were to die just before her birthday.'

'She won't do that,' said the other with confidence.

'How do you know?' demanded the other.

'Easy,' replied the confident one, 'God would never be so mean.'

Flaming arrow-prayer

A small girl was once asked by her mother to pray for fine weather in order that her grandmother's rheumatism might improve. When she got to her bed the lassie knelt down and prayed,

'Oh Lord, please make it hot for Grandma.'

'I KNOW YOU USED TO PLAY IN A CINEMA, BUT I DO WISH YOU WOULDN'T TAKE BOWS AFTER EVERY SERVICE.'

5
LAITY AT LARGE

It is easier to preach by the mile than to practise by the inch

There was once a celebrated preacher who had a brother in the medical profession whom he very much resembled. A man meeting the doctor brother one day and mistaking him for his clerical brother said,

'You preached a fine sermon last Sunday morning.'

'I'm afraid you're mistaken,' came the sharp reply, 'I am not the brother that preaches, I'm the one who practises.'

The devil meets his match

It is said that when Lloyd George was Prime Minister he went to a small Welsh town to speak on the Disestablishment of the Welsh Church. In introducing him, the Mayor, obviously a supporter, said, 'Ladies and Gentlemen, Mr Lloyd George has come to speak on Welsh Disestablishment and especially to answer the Bishop of St David's opposition to it. In my opinion, the Bishop of St David's is the greatest liar on the face of the earth. But, thank heaven, ladies and gentlemen, we have with us tonight one that is a match for him.'

Claws out in Commons

It was in 1873 that Disraeli launched a bitter and violent verbal attack on the harassing legislation of Mr Gladstone's Government. It was Bright who came to the rescue with the statement that, 'If such critics as Mr Disraeli had been alive at the time the Ten Commandments were issued, they would have condemned them as harassing legislation.'

Parsonic justice

When parsons rode round their parishes on horseback a little leg-pulling was not infrequent. There was a country squire in one parish who had lately been made a county magistrate and meeting his Rector one day on horseback he chided him gently that he was more ambitious than his Master who was content to ride upon an ass. The Rector was up to the occasion, however, since he replied; 'They cannot be gotten in these days, they've all been made Justices of the Peace.'

Passing bell

A bishop staying at a five star hotel in New Delhi during the Third Assembly of the World Council of Churches, had been pressing his bell for room service for about half an hour. Disgusted at the poor service, he had barely got into bed when the door opened and the waiter appeared. 'Did you ring, sir?'

'No,' came the gruff reply, 'I was tolling it. I thought you were dead.'

Fuss and fugue

Bishop Stubbs was once robing in the vestry of a church where a particularly noisy clergyman was fussing about the arrangements for the service. To add to this unwelcome din, the organ, in which the vicar took excessive pride, was playing its loudest. Said the Bishop, 'Could this not be done without all this organizing?'

Clothed in unrighteousness

Someone asked Charles James Fox the meaning of the passage in the Psalms, 'He clothed himself with cursing, like as with a garment.'

'The meaning,' he replied, 'is clear enough: the man had a *habit* of swearing!'

Purity in peril

It is said that the Gaelic poet Dugald Buchanan ultimately became a catechist because of a jest.

'What is your profession?' inquired a pious Highlander.

'As to that,' replied Buchanan, 'I have none particularly. My mind is very much as a sheet of white paper.'

'Then take care,' responded the inquirer, 'that the devil does not write his name upon it.'

Cure's crafty curtesy

'Oh vicar,' said the young woman in charge of the white elephant stall at the Sale of Work, 'why is it you haven't bought anything from my stall?'

'Well you see dear,' replied the vicar, who was to say the least, tight-fisted, 'I make a point of buying only from the stalls which are being staffed by plain looking ladies because it gives them a bit of encouragement.'

The young woman was thrilled with the compliment and forgave him all. So did all the other stall holders in the Sale of Work.

Death wish

On December 14th, 1917, Dean Inge made a speech to the 'League for Promoting International Friendship through the Churches.' In the speech he made some unpopular, but, as it happened, prophetic remarks. He prophesised that Britain would never be able to destroy German militarism; that there would be an armaments race which would lead to the suicide of Europe and that Britain would never be able to force Germany to adopt a democratic system. On December 17th, the Dean was attacked furiously for his speech in the newspapers and he received a mass of abusive letters. One from a lady read:

'I am praying for your death. I have been successful in two such cases.'

Stale-mate mates

There is a story which relates to a doctor in Whitby who stood as candidate for the vacant post of Dispensary Doctor. This candidate was opposed by the parish priest who worked strenuously against him; but despite this clerical opposition he was elected.

Unfortunately, however, the priest did not allow his antagonism to die with the election, but being a member of the Dispensary Committee he devised a plan to worry the doctor by issuing to all applicants an urgent or immediate ticket. No matter how trivial the illness or how late the hour, each applicant arrived at the doctor's house with an urgent ticket requiring attention, immediately. At length, the doctor tumbled to the priest's game and accordingly said to each patient, 'You are very ill, you had better see the priest at once.'

Seeing he got as good as he gave, the priest discontinued the use of the tickets and, in the end, the two became great friends.

Credo quia impossible

(*I believe it because it is impossible*)

The Reverend Doctor John Hildrop who became Rector of Watch near Ripon in 1734 was one day in company with a man who boasted that he would never believe anything which he did not understand.

'Ah!' said Hildrop, 'then I think you are likely to have the shortest creed of anyone in England.'

King's keys for lawyers

A certain barrister, Mr Curron, was once in conversation in a case with an Irish priest.

The barrister remarked, 'I hope, Father O'Leary, that when I die you have the key of heaven.'

'Why?' asked the priest.

'Well, replied Curron, 'because if you did you would let me in.'

'It would be easier for you,' retorted O'Leary, 'if I had the key of the other place, then I could let you out!'

Old Nick's not nackered

Lord Mureth, an Irish Judge, was trying a case where a veterinary surgeon was being sued for damages for having poisoned a valuable horse. Among the witnesses was a dispensary doctor who gave testimony to the effect that he had given five grains of the poison to a man with no ill effects and therefore twelve for a horse was not excessive.

'But Doctor,' said the Judge, 'wouldn't twelve kill the Devil himself?'

'I cannot say my Lord,' answered the Doctor pompously, 'I have never had the honour of prescribing for that patient.'

'Ah, no,' replied his Lordship, 'you never have, more's the pity, the old boy's still alive.'

Cow-licked

'Will I go to Heaven if I'm a very good girl?' asked a pupil of her Sunday School teacher.

'Yes,' came the reply.

'Will my cat go to Heaven as well,' she continued.

'No, I don't think animals will go.'

'Will the cows go to Heaven?'

'No,' said the teacher.

'Then,' asked the little girl, 'who will go to Hell for the milk?'

To live above with saints we love,
That will be bliss and glory;
To live below with saints we know,
Is quite a different story.

'Hands up all those children who want to go to heaven?' asked the inexperienced Sunday school teacher.

Every hand save one in the class reached for the sky.

'I notice your hand is not up Belinda. Don't you want to go to heaven?'

'Not likely, Miss,' she replied, 'not if this lot is going there!'

Condemned out of her own mouth

'Rachel,' snapped the Scripture mistress, 'you've not done a stroke of work in this lesson. I've warned you over and over again that the Devil finds work for idle hands to do. Take your roughbook and write that out fifty times.'

Calf love

A Sunday school teacher was attempting to draw a lesson from the character of the elder brother in the story of the Prodigal Son.

'But amidst all the rejoicing,' she said to the class, 'there was one to whom the preparation of the feast brought no joy: to whom the prodigal's return gave no pleasure at all, only bitterness; one who did not approve of the feast being held, and who did not want to attend it. I wonder, children, if any of you can tell me who that was?'

One little boy put up his hand and said, 'Oh please, the fatted calf.'

Those who can't, teach

Mr Richardson, headmaster of the village school, was of a haughty and pompous nature. Mr Hughes, a local farmer, concerned about his son's future, was being interviewed in the head's study on the subject of his son's career.

'What do you want the lad to be?' asked Mr Richardson with disdain.

'Well,' said the farmer, 'if he gets grace perhaps we'll make a Methodist minister of him.'

'Ah,' said the headmaster with a smirk, 'and what if he gets no grace, what then eh?'

'Then,' replied the farmer looking at the autocrat with Welsh fervour, 'he'll just have to become a school teacher like you.'

Divine non-intervention

It was in a trial conducted by Mr Justice Maulee that a man was found guilty of a very serious offence. The prisoner shouted from the dock, 'May God strike me dead my Lord, if I did it.'

The judge was silent for a while and then at length he said, 'As Providence has not seemed fit to interpose in your case, it now becomes my duty to pronounce upon you the lighter sentence of the law.'

Studying for her finals

Dropping into old Mary Jones' cottage one afternoon the local vicar found her reading her way laboriously through a passage of her Bible.

'Mary,' said the vicar, 'I always find you steeped in your Bible. Do you understand what you read?'

'Of course I do,' said she sharply.

'Well, I'm glad to hear that,' said her vicar, 'for I've been studying it all my life and I don't understand it all yet.'

'That's as maybe,' muttered the old woman, 'but if you are a blockhead there's no need to think that everyone else is like yourself.'

Oh Brother

A certain vicar was having a pretty rough time in his parish with members of his congregation. As he was returning home from service one Sunday he let his anger get the better of him, and in a conversation with his churchwarden he said, 'I have preached today to a congregation of asses.'

'Oh indeed,' said the churchwarden, whose sympathies lay with the congregation, 'is that why you addressed them as "Dearly beloved brethren".'

Larger than life

The story is told of John B. Stetson of the Globe Theatre, Boston, U.S.A., who was a theatrical magnate. One day he was watching a rehearsal of a Passion Play Spectacular and he demanded of the Stage Manager, 'Who are them fellows on the stage now?'

'Those,' said the Manager, 'are the twelve Apostles.'

'The devil they are,' said Stetson, 'what's the good of twelve on a stage this size; have fifty.'

I do not pin my faith upon your sleeve

There was a faith healer of Deal
Who said, 'Although pain is not real,
When I sit on a pin
And it punctures my skin,
I dislike what I fancy I feel.'

Edward Lear

Lost and found evangelism

In the West End of London at one time there was a man who used to dress up as a clergyman and go round whispering confidentially to people comforting remarks such as, 'Are you saved?' 'Hell is waiting for you.' 'Prepare to meet your God.' One night he sidled up to Sir Henry Irving as he walked down the street and whispered, 'Have you found the Lord?'

'No,' said Iriving, 'have you lost him? Because if you have I shall be delighted to join you in the search.'

Doubt dispeller

There was the case of the young man, a student at Cambridge, who brought to a professor, a fellow of his College, some difficulties and doubts about his faith which were worrying him.

'Difficulties! Doubt!' echoed the old man. 'Take a couple of glasses of port. If that don't dispel them, take two more, and continue the dose until you have found peace of mind.'

St Cedrics
NOTICES
come in
and have your
FAITH LIFTED

6
LIGHT-HEARTED LITURGICS

Eternal odours

A visitor to a very high church complained to the vicar that while he loved the service, he objected to what he called, "the stink of incense".

'I am sorry to hear that,' replied the vicar.

'Why?' asked the stranger.

'Because,' said the vicar firmly, 'there are only two stinks in the next world—Incense and Brimstone—and you will have to choose one of them!'

Customs like horses are made to be broken

Frederick Temple when Bishop of London made it a practice of taking the north-end position when celebrating the Holy Communion. This caused not a little ill-feeling in some churches. One incumbent ventured to expostulate mildly in the vestry before service. 'My Lord,' he said, 'it is the custom in this church for the celebrant to take the eastward position.'

'It will not be the custom this morning,' came the reply.

Soul agents for this district

'I was glad to see you in church last Sunday,' said a keen vicar to one of his parishioners who claimed to be an agnostic and who never came to church.

'Oh,' said the man, 'I only dropped in to get out of the rain.'

'You'll never get anywhere in life you know,' said the vicar, 'without religion.'

The man retaliated, 'Most of your members are hypocrites and only make a cloak of their religion!'

'Well,' contended the vicar, 'if you don't make a cloak of it, you've made an umbrella of it, and that's just as bad!'

Waiting for Old Nicko

In a South Wales parish two notable people, Squire Vaughan and Colonel Roberts vied to be the last to enter the church for service. It was the duty of the parish clerk to show them to their pews. It happened that the parson, the Reverend A. J. M. Green, entered his reading desk to start the service. He began the introduction, 'When the wicked man, turneth away—'

'He hasn't come yet, sir,' said the parish clerk in stentorian tones.

In their pews the congregation sat agog waiting to see which of the two gentlemen would appear first to claim the insult.

Tiring hymnody

William Stubbs, Bishop of Chester 1884–1889, abhorred many, and long hymns. After a particularly lengthy service, a Cheshire rector said to him, 'I hope my Lord, you thought the hymns appropriate?'

The service had taken almost two hours and Bishop Stubbs' patience was tried almost beyond endurance.

'Appropriate,' the Bishop answered testily, 'Oh dear yes, Rector! Yes, most emphatically.

"Yet saints their watch are keeping,
Their cry goes up, 'How long'?" '

Pride of place

'Church of the People,' 1867, records that 'at Cholderton, Wiltshire, is a pew 6 feet high, with glass windows in the door to enable the occupants to survey the congregation: all being fitted with sliding shutters.'

'At Branksea, Dorsetshire, there was one as large as a drawing-room, and magnificently furnished; it had a fire-place, and in addition, windows and blinds to secure privacy from the rest of the congregation.'

Great fleas have little fleas

'Paid to Good Wyfe Wells for salt to destroy the fleas in the Churchwarden's pew—6d.' Accounts of St Margaret's Church, Westminster, 1611.

First class compartments

The Bishop of Oxford, speaking to the Church Building Society in May, 1863, spoke of 'selfish pews, which showed that the spirit of the world had entered into the house of God—divided compartments which shut selfish respectability in, and shut poverty out. In order to escape the inconvenient damp and inconvenient draught, selfish respectability raised year by year a little higher the separating walls of the pew, lining it with a little fresh green baize, in order that the cherished neck might be preserved from the invading wind, and the tender inmate of the pew return home uncontaminated with rheumatism.' To which the eloquent Bishop might have added, 'and refreshed by unseen slumbers during the sermon.'

The pulpit trap

The Reverend E. H. L. Reeve, Rector of Stondon Massey, Essex, reported the following to the Reverend P. H. Ditchfield at the turn of the century.

The Rev Thomas Wallace was rector of Liston, in Essex, from 1783 onwards and it was a custom in those days for the parish clerk to announce the number of the hymn, which he usually did with a long preamble. This gave the officiating parson a chance of retiring to the vestry to exchange his surplice for his academic gown in which he preached.

On one occasion, Mr Wallace left his sermon at home. Whether he had gone to the rectory to look for it or whether he simply 'did a bunk', the clerk and congregation were not sure, but waited patiently and long for him to reappear, spinning out the hymn as much as possible to disguise their incumbent's retirement. When, however, they discovered that he was no longer in the vestry, they were understandably indignant at being let down.

The next Sunday the hymn before the sermon was not announced and the rector changed in the vestry in silence. When he had gone into the pulpit, the parish clerk slammed fast the pulpit door, and keeping his shoulder against it, called out to the congregation with a note of triumph, 'We've got him, boys; we've got him; now let us sing a hymn to the praise and glory of God.'

Sporting gesture

In the good old days when packs of hounds were a common sight in even the villages of Wales, a more sporting pack than that of Mr Panton of Ynysfor was hard to find. It was believed that he read prayers to his hounds, and it was also alleged that some of the Ynysfor hounds attended Llanfrothen church from time to time. One Sunday the old, very Welsh, rector, spotted them from his vantage point in his 'three decker' pulpit. 'William,' he called out, 'there is "docks" in the church.'

William, the clerk, who was fond of his sport, answered in awed reverence, 'Ynysfor dogs, sir.'

'Put them in the Yynysfor pew then,' said the reverend gentleman and carried on with his sermon like a good sportsman.

Whatever would St Paul say?

In Strype's *Life of Bishop Parker*, is a copy of a representation made to Queen Elizabeth I, concerning the irregular manner in which the service was conducted, and proceeds to state that, 'some ministers in a surplice, others without, some with a square cap, some with a round cap, some with a hat,' etc.

One of the Articles of Enquiry at Bishop Hackett's second triennial visitation in 1668 is, "Do your parishioners behave reverently in Church, men and youths with their hats off?" Similarly, Bishop Cosin, in his "Primary Visitation of Durham Cathedral 1662", speaks of "some who come into the quire in their furre and night gownes and sit with their hats on their heads at the reading of the lessons." In 1689 King William gave great offence because he would wear his hat in Church, and if he ever removed it during the litany, always put it back when the sermon began.

Unholy spirits

The Reverend R. S. Hawker, Vicar of Morwenstow, was told by one of his old parishioners how on one occasion the parish clerk allowed local smugglers to hide kegs of contraband under the pews and in the church tower.

'We bribed Tom Hockaday, the sexton, and we had the goods safe in the seats by Saturday night. The parson did wonder at the large congregation, for divers of them were not regular churchgoers at other times; and if he had known what was going on, he could not have preached a more suitable discourse, for it was,

"Be not drunk with wine, wherein is excess."

It was one of his best sermons; but, there, it did not touch us, you see; for we never tested anything but brandy and gin.'

The Auld Seceder Cat

There was a Presbyterian cat
Went forth to catch her prey;
She brought a mouse intill the house,
Upon the Sabbath day.
The minister, offended
With such an act profane,
Laid down his book, the cat he took
And bound her with a chain.

'Thou vile malicious creature,
Thou murderer,' said he,
'Oh do you think to bring to Hell
My holy wife and me?
But be thou well assured,
That blood for blood shall pay,
For taking of the mouse's life
Upon the Sabbath Day.'

Then he took doun his Bible,
And fervently he prayed,
That the great sin the cat had done
Might not on him be laid.
Then forth to exe-cu-ti-on,
Poor Baudrons she was drawn,
And on a tree they hanged her hie
And then they sung a psalm.

Anon.

Silent salute

One Christmas morning long ago a conversation was overheard in the church of Burgh-le-Marsh, Lincolnshire, between the vicar, one Parson Barnes and old Johnny Kelk, the parish clerk, who was justly proud of his fine alto voice. It was a bitterly cold and raw day and when Parson Barnes announced, 'Let us sing to the praise and glory of God, "Christians awake salute this happy morn".' Johnny Kelk yelled from the singing gallery at the west end, 'Noa! Us woan't.'

Parson Barnes yelled back angrily, 'Yes, we will.'

'Then you may sing un yoursen,' replied the old clerk. 'Us ain't a-going to crack our voices this cold marning o'er them high notes.'

The flea hunt

There was a period in the late nineteenth century when repeating tunes were used in worship and the lines or parts of them when fitted to these tunes produced the most astonishing and ludicrous effects.

One such was:

And catch the flee—
And catch the flee—
And catch the fleeting hours.

There were others too which raised poignant pathos to ridiculous sublimity.

My own sal
My own sal,
My own sal,
My own salvation's rock to praise.

My poor poll
My poor poll
My poor polluted heart.

And a chorus of women and girls in the west gallery sang desperately,

Oh for a man,
Oh for a man,
Oh for a mansion in the skies.

'As it was in the beginning'

The much loved Tom Clark, Archdeacon of Macclesfield, used to make it his custom to talk to churchwardens and especially to those who had been in office for a long time. One such was the local squire, a very old man, who had been warden of his parish for forty years.

'You must have seen lots of changes in the worship of the Church of England while you've been warden over the last forty years,' said the kindly Archdeacon.

'Yes,' came the reply, 'and I have resisted every one of them!'

National Pride

A Welsh Roman Catholic was asked what he thought of the new Mass.

'To be honest,' he said, 'I was very disappointed. They said it would be in the vernacular and it turned out to be in English.'

P. B. Shelley (revised)

In the *Church Times*, 1 October 1971, the Reverend C. M. Harrison, Aislaby Vicarage, Whitby, wrote:

> 'Sir,—The generous notices of the proposed liturgy contained in your issue of September 17 encourage me to hope that you will afford a like publicity to my own forthcoming Series III edition of some of the English poets.
>
> 'Like the Liturgical Commission, I and my fellow-editors have proceeded in our work by stages, as may be seen in our successive versions of the opening lines of '*Ode to a Skylark*', a poem by a man named Shelley of whom your readers may have heard, as he wrote a considerable number of years later than Cranmer. Our Series I was content to remove the obsolete second singular pronoun and accordingly read:
>
> *Hail to you, blithe spirit:*
> *Bird you never were.*
>
> However, further thought convinced us that the lines in this form still contained archaisms, and

that further work was required. Young people today are not in the habit of greeting each other with the word "Hail". The replacement of this word caused considerable discussion, our chairman, Canon Gasper, maintaining that the in-greeting was "Hiya," while a majority were of the opinion that this expression bordered on slang. "Blithe" clearly had to go together with the unnatural inversion in line 2. Accordingly, Series II read:

Good-morning, cheerful spirit:
You never were a bird.

'After deep study of this version, the editorial board still felt unhappy. It was by no means clear what the man Shelley intended by the word "spirit": while as for line 2, the board was in no doubt that in fact the skylark *was* a bird, and that the poet was either mistaken or deliberately misleading. Series III accordingly limits itself to the version:

Hey, lark:

'I trust the above example will interest you by its fruitful possibilities. An author named Shakespeare gives even wider scope for this treatment, and I can assure you that the Series III *Hamlet* will be entirely intelligible to the younger generation—or anyone else who should ever wish to read it in its new form.'

Knee-drill aids

A vicar had preached a long and very enthusiastic sermon on the revision of the Prayer Book in general and on the Series II services in particular.

'I can't understand what he's making so much fuss about,' said his oldest lady parishioner to her friend as they left the church. 'What's he making all the fuss about new prayer books for when what we want most is hassocks?'

Out of season

Canon Winston Hurlow, Rector of St Mary's without-the-Walls, Chester, tells of one of the Dukes of Westminster who objected very strongly to changes in the Church of England. He complained to his rector that he did not approve even if the changes which had been made in the Calendar of Lessons: 'Before the changes occurred the story of the Fiery Furnace always meant the beginning of the Grouse Season: now, dash it all, it comes in November.'

Let us sin

The people of a church had a shock when they collected the June issue of their Parish Magazine. There, for all to see because of a badly attached inset, was the first of a series of articles by Dr Gerald Knight, Director of the Royal School of Church Music. The heading was, "Let us Sin—and show we mean it!" The 'g' of 'sing' was obscured by the badly fixed staple. The magazine advertised a second instalment of the article as '"The right way to do it", to be published in three months time. Roll on September!'

Lay Retaliation

The Reverend John Heywood of St Margaret's, Dunham Massey (the church where the 'Red Dean' was a curate) tells of a certain remote Moorland daughter church in the old days to which the congregation travelled by charabanc for evening service. The chara' returned to the village one hour and a half later so it was important that the parson did not preach longer than fifteen minutes. A visiting parson, who didn't know of the difficulty, preached for half an hour. The sermon ended, up got the clerk and announced, 'We shall sing all the 'undred and seventy-six verses of the 'undred and nineteenth Psalm—we've missed the chara' 'cause he's preached all day, so we'll sing all night.'

Floundered upon a rock

When Rear Admiral Sir Cloudsley Shovel set out on the voyage which cost him his life (his ship was wrecked on the rocks off the coast of Scilly on 22 October, 1707), Thomas Tenison, Archbishop of Canterbury, composed a prayer for the success and safety of the expedition in which he had the misfortune to utter the plea that God would be for the fleet 'a rock of defence.'

Later, when a monument was erected in Westminster Abbey to the memory of the Rear Admiral, it was not surprising that the rocks on which his vessel foundered were known as 'The Bishop and his Clerks.'

'As Lambeth prayed, such was the dire event,
Else had we wanted now this Monument;
That God unto our fleet would be a rock,
Not did kind Heaven the fond petition mock.
To what the Metropolitan said then,
The Bishop and his Clerks replied, "Amen".'

A prayer too quickly answered

With folded hands, and lifted eyes,
'Have mercy, Heaven!' the parson cries,
'And on our sun-burnt, thirsty plains,
Thy blessings send in genial rains!'
The sermon ended and the prayers,
The parson to be gone prepares:
When with a look to brighten'd smiles—
"Thank Heaven, it rains,' cries farmer Giles—
'Rains!' quoth the parson, 'Sure you joke!
Rain! Heav'n forbid! I've got no cloak.'

Qui tacet consentire videtur

(*who is silent is held to consent*)

Donald Arden, Bishop of Malawi, wrote, 'We Anglicans make almost no use of this wonderful way of worship—being silent together before God. Anglicans too often turn the answer to the boy Samuel inside out: "Hear, Lord, for thy servant speaketh!" '

'——ARE YOU QUITE SURE THIS IS LITTLE TWITTERING IN-THE-WOLD?'

7
PASTORAL PECCADILLOS

Honest to God

Because of his incompatibility with the views held by certain professors of theology, a Scottish minister was moved to commend them in his prayers thus:

'O Lord, have mercy on these men; but if not, then send them to hell: and O Lord, send them quickly before they give further trouble to thy Church.'

Logical consequences are the scarecrows of fools and the beacons of wise men. (*Huxley*)

John Wesley was out walking when a swaggering 'gentleman' bumped into him on the pavement, and that with the insulting remark,

'I never make way for a fool.'

John Wesley stepped politely aside and with a bow, said,

'I always do.'

Give the devil his due

The Reverend Doctor Lawson of Selkirk was dining at a friend's house one evening when a gentleman in the party during his conversation gave free rein to somewhat extreme expressions. The climax came when the man said,

'The Devil take me.'

Dr Lawson got up from the company, ordered his carriage, and made for the door. His host insisted that he should stay as the dinner had only just begun, but nothing could stop the reverend gentleman. When pressed to give a reason for his leaving so early, he replied,

'That gentleman there,' pointing to the offender, 'has been praying that the Devil would take him and I have no wish to be present at the scene, so I beg to be allowed to depart.'

Wrong response

A guest staying at a Franciscan friary was awakened by an early morning tap at his door and the customary Latin greeting: *Dominus tecum* (The Lord be with you). With worldly-wise alacrity he replied,

'Thanks very much. Two lumps please and just leave it at the door.'

Yahweh

An elderly priest was told that there was a Jehovah's Witness at the vicarage door. 'Tell the man,' he said, 'that I am Jehovah's Witness in this parish.'

All lost! to prayers, to prayers! all lost!

(*Shakespeare: The Tempest I.i*)

The vicar had called to see one of his men who had been taken sick, and before leaving the house he knelt by the bedside saying to the family,

'Let us offer up a prayer for the sick man.'

In great alarm, the patient cried, 'O Lord, has it come to that?'

Best 'vishes

Some young parsons become pettily pedantic over the observance of saints' days and festivals in the Church's year and tend to carry their enthusiasm over into their ordinary everyday activities. One such, always had to drag the practice into his letter writing by bringing his missive to a close with, 'Have a good St Andrew's Day', or 'Best wishes for Advent.' This custom harmed no one until, when writing to his bishop on January 1st he unthinkingly closed with, 'Have a good Circumcision'.

Thou shalt not covet the vicar's living

A vicar, long ill, who had treasured up wealth,
Told his curate each Sunday to pray for his health;

Which oft having done, a parishioner said,
That the curate ought rather to wish he were
  dead.
'By my troth,' said the curate, 'let credit be given,
I ne'er prayed for his death—but I have for his
  living.' *Jerrold's Epigrams.*

Oh where oh where is the incense pot?
It's down in the aisle 'cos it's too damned hot.

It once came to the notice of Bishop Creighton that a London vicar was using incense, a practice to which the vicar seemed to attach the utmost importance, and the Bishop had to administer a rebuke.

'But my Lord,' protested the incense-swinging vicar, 'I have the cure of ten thousand souls.'

'Quite so,' replied the Bishop, 'but you need not cure them with smoke, like so many kippers!'

'Happy those who have only to cultivate the Lord's vineyard, instead of repairing the hedge which the wild boar out of the wood has broken down.' (*E. B. Pusey*)

What legions of fables and whimsical tales
Pass current for gospel where priestcraft prevails!
Our ancestors thus were most strangely deceiv'd;
What stories and nonsense for truth they
  believ'd!
But we, their wise sons, who these fables reject,
Even truth now-a-days, are too apt to suspect:
From believing too much the right faith we let
  fall;
So now we believe—troth! just nothing at all.
(*Anon*)

The conversion of the Ethiopian eunuch
(*As it might have turned out today*)

An angel of the Lord said to Philip—'Get up and go south down the road which runs from Jerusalem to

Gaza, out in the desert.' And Philip arose and pulled forth his diary and said to the angel—'I have a committee meeting at 10 and at 11.30 I have to be at Bethany, for a plenary session of the elders, I couldn't really make it until after lunch.'

With apologies to St Luke

Comprehensive prayer

'O Lord, please make all the bad people good, and the good people interesting.'

Ich Dien (*I serve—I deal*)

The 'Baccarat scandal' of 1891, in which Sir William Gordon-Cumming was accused of cheating when the Prince of Wales held the bank during a game at Tranby Croft, Doncaster, set Welsh nonconformist tongues wagging and pens writing. The prince was subpoenaed to appear as a witness for Sir William in the case that opened on June 1 1891 and lasted for seven days. Sir William lost the case and the Prince got much of the backwash. The Prince not only played baccarat but one of his best friends was labelled a cheat.

Nonconformists up and down the country were holding meetings. 'The Welsh Baptists declared that the Prince was fostering "immoral habits", and the Wesleyans "bitterly regretted that the heir to the throne should be given to one of the worst forms of gambling . . . and that he took about with him counters for the game".'

Virginia Cowles records that in the 'Review of Reviews' the editor calculated that 880,000,000 prayers had been said for His Royal Highness since his birth and pointed out that the only answer from the Almighty seemed to be a baccarat scandal.

(*Edward VII and His Circle*—Virginia Cowles
Hamish Hamilton 1956)

A soft touch

Thinking to have a little fun, a soldier spotted a Salvation Army lassie on duty at a street corner. He strolled over to her.

'Will you pray for me?' he asked sarcastically. She reached up, placed a hand on his head and, in a voice plainly heard by his pals, said,

'O Lord, make this young man's heart as soft as his head.'

Perils of prayer

It was on a fishing trawler in the North Sea, when a very severe storm was raging, that the skipper said to the crew, 'Does anyone here know how to pray?'

The youngest member of the crew said, 'I do Skipper'.

'Right ho my lad, you go ahead and pray and the rest of us will put on life jackets. We happen to be one short.'

Gott-trunkener Mensch (*A God-intoxicated man*)

Members of a branch of the Church of England Men's Society in a small country parish were having a discussion about war. They were talking in particular about the Second World War.

'You see,' said one old man who had served his time in the Great War, 'our soldiers were bound to win because they prayed to God before going into battle.'

'Ah,' said a young man, 'but the Germans prayed too; they had a motto, "God is on our side".'

'Well there was no point in the Germans praying,' retaliated the old soldier, 'because God couldn't possibly have understood that foreign language.'

A holy hindrance

A visitor on looking round a church one day went to enter the chancel whereupon he was told by a rather officious lady,

'You must not go in there.'

'Why not?' asked the visitor.

'I'm put here to stop you,' said the lady.

'Oh! I get it,' said the visitor, 'you're what is called the *rude* screen.'

Advisory prayer

A negro, framed for his laziness, found salvation at a revivalist meeting. Invited to pray, he said,

'Use me O Lord, use me in Thy work,' paused, and then added, 'I mean, of course, O Lord, in an advisory capacity.'

May the Lord preserve you

A Bishop who had only recently been appointed to a Missionary Diocese had not managed to learn much of the native language before being called upon to give the blessing at a service in the Cathedral Church: donning his mitre he pronounced, as he thought, 'May the Lord preserve you,' in the native language. A gasp of horror went up from the congregation for his blessing in fact expressed the wish,

'May the Lord pickle you for ever.'

8
PEWNAMICS

Procrastination is the thief of time (*Young*)

A certain long-winded vicar was given the job of introducing a subject on which a well-known bishop in the Church of England was to speak. The introduction, like most introductions, could have been completed in a few sentences, but the long-winded vicar went on for about half an hour and dealt with the subject very extensively. As he sat down he turned to the Bishop and said, 'I hope my Lord, that I have not encroached upon your time.'

'Time,' growled the Bishop under his breath, 'you have encroached upon Eternity.'

Brief encounter

Overheard outside the parish Church after Mattins, which had started at 11 am, as the clock struck 12.30 pm.

'Yes, it was the vicar this morning, more's the pity. When the curate preaches and says, "and now to conclude," he does conclude but when the vicar says, "and lastly," he lasts.'

Sound advice

A curate once asked a former Bishop of Oxford, Dr Stubbs, 'What ought I to preach about?' After a pause the Bishop replied, 'About God and about twenty minutes.'

Over their heads

On one occasion that great preacher Spurgeon was listening to a sermon of a very high academic calibre. He remarked to the young preacher, 'Your Lord and Master sent you out to feed sheep: you preach as if you were feeding giraffes.'

Try to look as much like an inspired idiot as you can

Dr Spurgeon, when holding a sermon class for students, gave the following advice: 'When you speak of Heaven, let your face light up, let it be irradiated by a heavenly gleam, let your eyes shine with reflected glory; but when you speak of Hell—your ordinary face will do.'

Failure to strike root

Rising to make his maiden speech in the House of Lords, the Earl of Rochester during the reign of Charles the Second, said,

'My Lords, I rise this time for the first time—the very first time. My Lords, I divide my speech into four branches.'

Here there was a long embarrassing pause.

'My Lords,' the Earl groaned, 'if ever I rise again in this House, you may cut me off root, branches and all for ever.'

Evaporated sermons

A newly-appointed vicar was spending his first day in his rural parish walking around in order to become conversant with the general lay-out of the place. As he passed by one cottage he was accosted by an old man leaning on the garden gate. 'Are you our new vicar?' asked the local, to which the vicar replied in the affirmative. 'I hope you're a better preacher than the last one we 'ad! What are you preaching on this coming Sunday?'

The vicar answered, 'I am preaching on the Milk of Human Kindness.'

With a snort the old man replied, 'Well I hope that it's the condensed type.'

Feed my cats

When Bishop of Truro, Benson wrote to his wife from Convocation House 2 June, 1880:

'My two sermons on Sunday are very oppressive to my soul—not the writing but the shortening—for these Londoners won't stand more than 25 minutes and I can't work anything out in that time. And really these are days when one ought to try to make people see. It's no use stroking them while they stand purring; or making feints at them while they stand "spitting". It's time to put facts and reasons before them.'

'I do not advise any young minister to preach *extempore* until he has preached three or four hundred written sermons; until he has been at least three or four years preaching.'

(*Charles Simeon*)

It is quite often the case that parsons who are not great orators have a high opinion as to their own preaching prowess. One such curate was preaching the sermon at evening service when Archbishop Temple was present. In the vestry after the service the Archbishop greeted him. Said the parson, 'I always pledge myself to preach in the evening *extempore*.'

Lifting up his hands Archbishop Temple said quietly, 'Kneel down and I'll absolve you of your pledge.'

I have lost my portmanteau
I pity your grief.
It contained all my sermons
I pity the thief. (*Jerrolds Epigrams*)

Dr Robert Gillian was appointed to succeed Dr Laurance Lockhart as minister of Inchinnan. When he took up residence Dr Lockhart wrote to him expressing the hope that the manuscripts and sermons he had forgetfully left behind in the attic were kept free from damp. Dr Gillian answered, 'The manuscripts are quite dry, *especially the sermons*.'

The bare truth

It was an Irish parson preaching on the Prodigal Son who confused his congregation somewhat when he said,

'A lad left home with good intentions but got into bad company. He had to pawn his overcoat in order to raise money to feed himself; later his jacket and shirt had to go in the same way; yet again he needed money, so he had to pawn what remained, his trousers, vest and pants; then he came to himself...'

Allegory is a dangerous aid

A somewhat dramatic preacher in a Welsh church was trying to describe to his congregation the terrors of hell.

'My friends,' he said, 'you've seen iron coming out of a furnace, haven't you? It comes out white hot, sizzling and hissing. Well, they use that stuff for ice-cream in the place of which I've been speaking.' It was the same parson who, when trying to describe the Holy Spirit's continual presence with the faithful, said to the congregation, 'You've all walked down the street past the fish and chip shop and the lovely aroma of fish and chips comes out to meet you and clings round you, and even when you've left the chip shop behind you, you can still smell the fish and chips; well, the Holy Spirit is like that.'

Oh boy!

A well-known preacher on one occasion announced that instead of preaching as he usually did by taking a text and expounding it, he would give a series of sermons on the boys of the Bible, commencing with

Samuel, the prophet-boy; then David, the shepherd boy and so on.

'That's a good idea,' said one of his colleagues on the staff, 'but don't forget to include Methuselah the old-boy and Esau the broth-of-a-boy.'

Darken our lightness

A young curate who had made a study of the Reverend Doctor Spooner got somewhat caught up with his subject and announced from the pulpit one Mattins,

'Yes, my friends, it is more difficult for a rich man to enter heaven than it is for a camel to go through the knee of an idol.'

The vicar of hell

'How are you getting on with your new vicar?' asked the churchwarden from a neighbouring parish, of a faithful worshipper.

'Oh quite well, but he's nowhere near as good as the last one, especially when it comes to preaching about hell. The last man described it and preached about it so well you would think that he had been born, bred and reared there.'

Fed up

A new minister was sent to preach at a chapel in an isolated part of the West Country. It was his first solo appearance, so he went to a lot of trouble preparing his sermon and arranging the worship. When he got to the chapel he found he had a congregation of one. Being a bit nervous he decided to consult the congregation about whether he ought to go ahead with the service or not.

'That I don't roightly know,' said the congregation. 'Oi'm only a cow hand around these parts and Oi haven't got much eddercation—but Oi can tell ee this—if Oi went into the field to feed the cows and only one of un turned up, Oi'd certainly feed un.'

An hour and a half later the preacher went to the west door to ask the congregation if he had enjoyed the service.

'Well Oi couldn't roightly say,' he was told, 'Oi'm only a cow hand around these parts and Oi haven't got much eddercation—but I can tell ee this, if Oi went into the field to feed the cows and only one of un turned up, Oi certainly wouldn't give un the whole load!'

A prophet put in his place

An old Scots country parson preached a series of very lengthy sermons on the Hebrew prophets and their relevance in the life of his day. At last he reached Haggai, and having held forth for some unconscionable time on his importance and influence, asked the rhetorical question, 'And what place shall we give Haggai?'

Sick with impatience, a man in the back pew jumped up and cried out with relief, 'He can have mine, I'm off home!'

All in all, he's a problem must puzzle the devil.

(*Robert Burns*)

A vicar once began his sermon, 'My dearly beloved brethren, you will find the subject of our observations this evening in the First Epistle General of Peter, the fifth chapter, the eighth verse, and in these words, "The Devil, as a roaring lion, walketh about seeking whom he may devour." Now my brethren, with your permission, we will divide our text into four heads. First we shall endeavour to ascertain who the devil he was; secondly, we will look at the geographical position, namely, where the devil was he going?; thirdly, and this is of a personal nature—we will ask ourselves, who the devil he was seeking?; fourthly, and lastly, my beloved brethren, we shall endeavour to solve a problem which has never been solved to this day, namely, what the devil was he roaring at?'

Circumnavigating metaphysics

The village postman was talking to Walter Pryce the blacksmith on the way home from church where they had listened to a very learned discourse by the rector.

Stan asked Walter what the meaning of metaphysics was.

'Well you see Stan, when the congregation that's listening does not know what the parson is speaking about, and when the parson who's speaking doesn't know what he means, that's metaphysics.'

Biblical business sense

A young agnostic was having a go at a clergyman and tried to put him on the spot by asking, 'How do you reconcile St Matthew's version of our Lord's words, "Are not two sparrows sold for a farthing", with St Luke's, "Are not five sparrows sold for two farthings?"'

The clergyman with a twinkle replied, 'Because you get them cheaper if you take a quantity.'

Sinner deterrent

A minister applying to be a prison chaplain was being interviewed by the selection committee of the prison board. One of the selectors said,

'I have no objections to the applicant since I understand he has preached his church empty already, and if he is as successful in prison perhaps he will preach that vacant as well.'

The Old Testament to the rescue

The Earl of Stair when Ambassador in Holland used to entertain the foreign ministers regularly; even

France was not exluded although hostilities were then commencing between the two countries. On one occasion the French minister proposed a toast to, 'The rising sun,' referring to his King, Louis XIV, and this was drunk by the whole company. Baron de Riesbach, the Austrian ambassador, appreciating the humour of the occasion, asked the company to toast, 'The moon and fixed stars', in compliment to the Empress Queen. All eyes were now fixed on the English Ambassador, who rose and asked the company to drink to his master in the toast of, 'Joshua, the son of Nun, who made the sun and moon to stand still.'

Holy Moses!

During a parliamentary election when religious piety in Wales was at its highest, a candidate with little or no religious leaning or knowledge, was asked by a man in the audience, 'Are you in favour of the Decalogue?'

Finding himself out of his depth he answered with naive honesty, 'Mr Chairman, I am compelled to say that this important matter is new to me, but I give my word that if elected, it will receive my immediate and favourable consideration.'

Dr Jowett, when Master of Balloil, told Margot Asquith, 'My dear child, you must believe in God in spite of what the clergy tell you.'

It was Bishop Bloomfield who used to tell the story of how, after a lapse of many years, he visited the University Church at Cambridge. There he met the verger who remembered him as an undergraduate.

'Yes,' said the old verger when the Bishop commended him on his healthy appearance, 'I have much to be grateful for. I have heard every sermon that has been preached in this church for fifty years, and I am a Christian still!'

9
STUTTERING STRATEGICS

Cross Baring

The hymn 'Onward Christian Soldiers', was written in 1865 by that high churchman and historian, Baring-Gould. It is said that on one occasion when it was being sung as a processional hymn, an evangelical objected to the cross being carried at the head of the choir. The author suggested that instead of singing, 'With the cross of Jesus going on before', the people might well sing instead, 'left behind the door'.

Fishy question

A nervous curate who was prone to spoonerism was talking to a member of his congregation who happened to be a very elegant young lady. She had been away on holiday and as her father was a keen fisherman, they had been on a fishing expedition.

'Did you get any fishing when you were on holiday?' he asked.

'Oh, yes,' she replied sweetly, 'quite a lot, but only coarse fishing, mostly perch and chub you know. Neither of them much good for eating actually.'

'Quite so,' said the curate obviously out of his depth, 'now which do you prefer, church or pub?'

Hypothetical heredity

'I'm Church of England like my father and grandfather before me,' said the old farmer to a proselytizing Jehovah's Witness.

'That's a weak argument to use,' simpered the door-knocking fanatic; 'suppose your father had been a fool and your grandfather a fool, what would you be then?'

'One of your lot,' snapped the old farmer as he firmly shut the door.

Ham and egg parable

A hen and a pig passed a church with a poster which read, 'How can we help the poor?' The hen hit on the idea of providing a ham-and-egg breakfast.

'It's easy for you to suggest that,' the pig replied testily. 'For you that's just a contribution, but for me it would mean total commitment!'

My penny of observation.

(*Shakespeare: Love's Labour Lost III i*)

It was Archdeacon Leslie Fisher of Chester who told the story of a certain Welsh parson who was preaching on S.P.C.K. He took as his main illustration the way in which Mary Jones saved up to buy her Bible. Said the parson, leaning over the pulpit,

'My friends, Mary Jones didn't spend a penny for six whole months while she saved up for her Bible.'

Bishop Lazarus

All his life Bishop Winnington-Ingram had been a great money-raiser for the church. He used to claim that when he died his epitaph would be:

'Last of all, the beggar died also!'

Comforting creditor

In a San Francisco church many years ago the man taking the collection plate around offered it to a young man who shook his head violently. 'But you must give something,' said the man with the plate. 'You've heard what the minister said: it is your duty.'

The Young man replied, 'My money belongs to my creditors.'

'But who is our greatest creditor?' asked the collector.

'To whom we owe most,' said the young man.

'Surely that is God!'

'Quite true,' was the reply, 'but just now He's not crowding me so much as the others.'

Graded giving

If ought thou hast to give or lend,
This ancient Parish Church befriend,
If poor, but still in spirit willing,
Out with thy purse and give a shilling;
But if its depths should be profound,
Out with thy purse and give a pound.
Look for no record to be given,
But trust to thy receipt in Heaven.

(*Parish Church of St Nicholas*, ***Brighton***)

Coin count

In a country parish where a town parson was taking a locum, a recent innovation had been an early Sunday celebration of the Holy Communion. The parson was shocked to the core when the verger came up with the collection at the offertory and said, 'There be twelve present but only ten 'as paid up.'

The dead end

A leading stewardship director was campaigning in a somewhat dangerous fashion at a meeting of leading parishioners in a Cheshire parish. After an enthusiastic address on Christian stewardship he departed from his usual procedure and issued an open challenge.

'Is there any businessman here who will commit himself to giving his parish church two hundred pounds a year?'

A sombrely dressed man jumped up and said, 'I will.'

'Bless you sir,' said the stewardship director, 'and may your business treble in the coming year.'

A dreadful silence crept over the hall and it was obvious that the meeting had died on him.

'What have I said to deserve this?' he whispered to the vicar in the chair.

'Nothing really; it's just that the volunteer is also the parish undertaker.'

Light hearted doctrine

Bishop Stubbs when going for a holiday was full of the *joie de vivre* and not a little naughtiness. On his arrival at Oxford station an over-attentive porter rushed up to him to get the job of carrying his luggage.

'How many articles, my Lord?' he asked.

'Thirty-nine,' replied the bishop with unmoved countenance.

The porter set to work to remove the episcopal baggage from the carriage and proceeded to count the various 'articles'. He was puzzled, however, to find himself well short of the full compliment of thirty-nine. He reported, 'Very sorry, my Lord, I can only find fifteen.'

'Ah!' said the bishop, 'you must be a Dissenter!'

Divine lock-out

There is the story of the coloured man who was very anxious to join a certain exclusive South African church but in view of apartheid among the congregation the minister considered it wise to put him off with an excuse. Some days later they met, whereupon the coloured man said, 'Ah prayed de good Lord and he sent me an answer after ah saw you.'

'Is that so,' said the minister, 'and what did the Lord say?'

'Well, sah, he asked me which church ah wished to join and ah told him it was yours. Then he says to me, "Ho! Ho! that church! you sure can't get in der. I know you can't 'cos I' been trying to get in dat church myself for ten years and ah couldn't!" '

Ecumenical encounter

A young man, a Roman Catholic, met a Presbyterian girl, and they decided to have what is now known as an ecumenical encounter. First the young man took the girl along to Mass at the Roman Catholic church, and as the service progressed, explained it all to her point by point.

The following week the girl reciprocated and they both went along to the Prebyterian chapel. As the beadle walked down the aisle carrying the Bible, its significance as a symbol that the Scripture was central in the Presbyterian denomination was explained to the young Roman. Presently, the minister went into the pulpit to preach, took off his watch and rested it on the edge of the puplit to gauge the length of his sermon.

Whispered the girl to her companion, 'That,' pointing to the watch, 'is of no significance whatever.'

Ecumenical stalemate

Cardinal Vaughan and Dr Adler, Chief Rabbi, were sitting side by side at a luncheon.

'Dr Adler,' said the Cardinal, with a twinkle in his eye, 'when may I have the pleasure of helping you to some ham?'

The Rabbi's reply was as quick as a flash. 'At your Eminence's wedding!'

Commanders of the Faithful

The Pope he is a happy man,
His palace is the Vatican,
And there he sits and drains his can:
The Pope he is a happy man.

I often say when I'm at home
I'd like to be the Pope of Rome.

And then there's Sultan Saladin,
The Turkish Sultan full of sin;
He has a hundred wives at least,
By which his pleasure is increased:
I've often wished, I hope no sin,
That I were Sultan Saladin.

But no, the Pope no wife may choose,
And so I would not wear his shoes;
No wine may drink the proud Paynim,
And so I'd rather not be him:
My wife, my wine, I love, I hope,
And would be neither Turk nor Pope.

William Makepeace Thackeray

Down with the poet

The following inscription had been placed over the door of a school in the North of Ireland in the early days of this century:

'Tis education forms the common mind,
Just as the twig is bent, the tree's inclined.
POPE'

Very shortly after, an indignant parent wrote underneath it,

'A pope indeed! We'll have no pope nor popery in this parish.'

Vulgate vulgarized

Geoffrey Wheeler tells of a canon in the diocese of Coventry whose neighbouring Anglican vicar was a high churchman of the pedantic type. So pretentious was he in fact, and 'catholic', that the canon took a particular dislike to him. The canon's Roman Catholic neighbour, on the other hand, was a great friend and not at all bigoted where his faith was concerned. The canon and the Roman Catholic priest were walking together through the City one day when the high church priest came towards them. He stopped, bowed to the pair and said, 'Dominus vobiscum'. The pair did not stop but as they passed him the Roman Catholic priest responded, 'Agatha Christie.'

Fraternal fraternization

In a town where faltering steps towards unity were only just beginning, the Roman Catholic priest, the Anglican vicar, the Baptist and Methodist ministers, decided to form themselves into a Fraternal and that the first meeting should be at the vicarage. The vicar, realizing that the first meeting would be a little strange and somewhat tense, asked his wife to bring in a tray of drinks to loosen things up.

His colleagues duly arrived and the vicar's wife, with that extra brush of the hair and a little more lipstick than usual, glided into the room with the drinks' tray. 'A glass of whisky please,' was the request from the Roman Catholic.

'My denomination does not exactly approve,' said the Methodist, 'but just a little sherry won't do any harm.'

Approaching the Baptist Minister with tray in hand she was fixed with an almost fanatical stare. 'Madam,' he said, 'I would rather commit adultery than let a drop of alcohol pass my lips!'

Going up to his hostess the Roman Catholic priest said with smooth gentility, 'Would you mind if I put my glass of whisky back? I didn't realize there was an alternative!'

'REMEMBER, VICAR, IT WAS ST. PAUL WHO SAID, "TAKE A LITTLE WINE FOR THY STOMACH'S SAKE"'.

10
TIPPLERS, TEMPTATION, AND TEMPERANCE

A toast

God made man
Frail as a bubble,
God made Love,
Love made trouble;
God made the vine,
Was it a sin,
That man made wine
To drown trouble in?

'There goes the parson, oh illustrious spark! And there, scarce less illustrious, goes the clerk.' (*Cowper*)

It was a sad occasion when the vicar found his parish clerk very much the worse for drink one night. Next morning when the vicar took him to task the parish clerk tried to excuse his intoxicated state by blaming the generosity of the parishioners.

'But, Stan,' said the vicar, 'I can go into town on market day without coming back intoxicated.'

'Yes, sir,' said Stan, 'that be so: but then, you see, I be so popular!'

The best whisky can be spoilt by too much water

There was an old parish priest who very much enjoyed his glass of whisky. His colleagues in the ministry noticed that he always drank his glass with one eye shut. One young curate was bold enough to ask the reason for this eccentric habit.

'Well, my boy,' said the old vicar, 'it's like this. The sight of a glass of whisky makes my mouth water and I don't want to over dilute it.'

Here's to old Adam's crystal ale,
Clear, sparkling and divine,
Fair H_2O long may you flow,
We drink your health (in wine).

A vicar had been asked to preach a temperance sermon when he was visiting a neighbouring church and he began his sermon by saying,

'There are only two drinks mentioned in the Book of Psalms; one is "wine that maketh glad the heart of man" and the other is water where "the wild asses quench their thirst". You may take your choice.'

'The Clergy will dine at the Mitre,
The Vintners at the Three Tuns,
The Usurers to the Devil will goe,
And the Fryars to the Nunnes.'

(*From the Roxburgh Ballads*)

The *Cardinal's Hat* is a very good inn
And so is the *Puritan's Head*;
But I know a sign of a wine, a wine
That is better when all is said.
It is whiter than Venus, redder than Mars,
It was old when the world begun;
For all good inns are moons and stars,
But the *Mermaid* is their Sun.

Chorus

They are all alight like moons in the night,
But the *Mermaid* is their Sun.

Therefore when priest or parson cries
That inns like flowers increase,
I say that mine inn is a church likewise,
And I say to them, 'Be at peace!'
An host may gather in dark St Paul's
To salve their souls from sin;
But the light may be where 'two or three'
Drink wine in the *Mermaid Inn*.

Chorus
The light may be where 'two or three'
Drink wine in the *Mermaid Inn*.

Alfred Noyes

Asininity's choice

At a temperance meeting one of the speakers put before the audience a question:

'If I had a pail of water and placed it alongside a bucket of beer and a donkey was brought in, which do you think he would take?' From the audience, a fellow noted for his tippling, stood up and said,

'The water of course.'

'Why do you think he would make that choice?' asked the speaker from the platform with a note of triumph in his voice.

'Because he's an ass,' came the deliberate reply.

None but a child or a drunken man tells the truth (*Old Suffolk saying*)

'Of course,' said the vicar, who was chairman of the local temperance association, when engaging a new verger, 'you are strictly sober?'

'Yes, your Reverence,' came the applicant's cheerful reply, 'very often.'

We shall sing, 'Little drops of water,' and this time put more spirit into it

Temperance can be taken to absurd limits. On one occasion a new ship was to be launched by the mayor of a ship-building town but one of his colleagues on the council, a man of much influence, objected to a bottle of alcholic beverage being smashed over the bows. It was the mayor's chaplain who came to the rescue by pointing out to the bigotted T.T. councillor that launching a ship with a bottle of wine was really a lesson in temperance indicating that after the first bottle the ship took to water and never left it again.

Tippling tip

A casual church attender had got the idea that water from the River Jordan would be needed for the baptism of his new baby. He obtained some in a flask and taking it to church, handed it to the verger. Before he could get in a word of explanation the verger whispered,

'No, not now, sir, I'll have that when the service is over.'

Pub-licity

When Mr Guinness, who later became Lord Iveagh, contested a Dublin seat in an election, his opponents brought out a poster which had a strong Biblical flavour:

'Those that are not with us are *agin us*'

(*He brews XX and XXX*)

This business will never hold water

(*Colley Cibber*)

'Do you drink?' a vicar once asked a parishioner whose manner was somewhat truculent and whose red nose suggested that he hit the whisky bottle fairly frequently.

'That's my business,' retorted the parishioner.

'Any other?' asked the vicar.

Here's champagne to our real friends and real pain to our sham friends

Old Parson John, as he was affectionately known, was fond of his glass. A little too fond and too often, but his people loved him and perpetually forgave him his indiscretions of intemperance; all except Miss Philipson of "The Towers", that is. An incorrigibly self-righteous and respectable spinster and pillar of the church, (and a niece of the late Archdeacon), she never ceased to be scandalized by his wine-bibbing.

Coming upon him teetering affably through the churchyard one evening, she called out scathingly, 'Drunk again, Vicar?'; to which Parson John responded with sympathetic understanding,

'Never mind, my dear, so am I.'

Food for the birds

An ordinand, who shall remain nameless, was out for the day with the Hereford City Police on their annual outing. A party of them decided to have a picnic near one of the villages they were visiting. They sent the ordinand, the son of one of the police inspectors, into the village to buy the wherewithall. He returned staggering under a burden of beer bottles and a long loaf of french bread.

'Good lad,' said the only sergeant in the party, 'he's even remembered the sparrows.'

Glass distinction

Bishops these days are often interviewed for television programmes. One very forgetful bishop is never certain whether he is being interviewed by B.B.C. or I.T.V. until he is offered a drink before the programme starts. At the B.B.C. the request is inevitably, 'Sweet or dry sherry, my Lord?', but he knows he is on the other channel when someone says, 'What will you have with your gin?'

'THEIR WING THREE-QUARTER DOESN'T LOOK MUCH, BUT HE'S THE GREATEST WHEN IT COMES TO CONVERTING!'

11
SPORTFUL SPORTMANSHIP

To hell and back by rail

'Where are you off to Jim m' boy?' asked the Irish Catholic priest of one of his congregation whom he met outside a railway station.

'I'm off to the races, your reverence,' was the reply.

'Then do you know Jim m' boy that you're off to hell?' censured the priest severely.

'Ach! and what if I am, sure an' it will be a new experience. And anyway, I've got a return ticket.'

'God could have produced a better berry than a strawberry, but He never did, and He could have put it into the mind of man to invent a better game than cricket, but He never did.'

(*Horace Walpole*)

It was Doctor Talbot, sometime Bishop of Winchester, who used to say that his excellent health was due to the fact that he had played cricket all his life. While Bishop of Winchester, he was taking part in a village match where the bowling was frenzied, and after receiving a ball which was very wide, the Bishop suggested to the bowler that he should keep them in the parish. Accidentally, the next ball came straight as a die and, rising swiftly, caught the Bishop in his stomach. Said the bowler,

'I do believe that was in the Diocese, my Lord.'

A Rot Amongst the Bishops, or a terrible wind in the diocesan see

(*with apologies to Thomas Stirry* 1641)

Diocesan cricket matches are becoming more and more popular in the Church of England. On one occasion the bishop of a diocese was playing for the first eleven against the second eleven. The bishop was the opening bat and no sooner than he had taken his place at the wicket than a swift delivery, which was helped by a strong wind, beat him completely, enabling the ball to graze the bail which fell. The bishop made no attempt to leave his wicket but bent down, picked up the bail and replaced it carefully, saying meaningfully to the umpire, who was one of his archdeacons,

'Very windy today Mr Archdeacon.'

'Yes, my Lord, it is,' said the archdeacon quietly, 'but I'm not, and you're out!'

United we win

A certain Hampshire clergyman was an umpire, and on a Sunday morning in 1903 he made the following announcement from the pulpit:

'On Saturday next we play the return match with Slocumb Magna. I shall umpire on that occasion, when I trust that our united endeavours will meet with success.'

All at sevens and eights

A parson who had intended preaching on the text, 'And immediately the cock crew and Peter went out and wept bitterly,' on the Sunday after the Oxford and Cambridge Boat Race, was so distracted that when he got into the pulpit he gave out his text as, 'Peter coxed and the crew wept bitterly.'

Cheap labourer wanted—ability to preach, pray, and bowl, an asset

Bowls has always been a popular game with the clergy and many great Prelates and Divines have taken to the woods. Among these we hear of Calvin, Archbishop Cranmer, Knox, and even Bishop Atterbury of Rochester.

Writing of the clergy in 1685 Macaulay stated: 'A large proportion of those divines who had no benefices, or whose benefices were too small to afford a comfortable revenue, lived in the houses of laymen. ... A young levite might be had for his board, a small garret, and £10 a year, and might not only perform his own professional functions, might not only be ready in fine weather for bowls, and in rainy weather for shove-board, but also save the expense of a gardener or groom.'

Them's fighting words

The wife of a boxer brought her son to be baptised. The vicar asked what the name was going to be.

'We've decided to call him Archibald Halgernon,' announced the mother.

'My word,' said the parson, 'that seems to be a strange and high-flown name to give a young lad; what made you choose it?'

'We've done it to help him vicar,' was the answer. 'In the street where we live this kid is going to have to fight with a name like that!'

A Scots Act of Parliament of 1457 decreed 'that the Fateball and Goff be crijit doune and not usit.' This was on the basis that it hindered the practice of archery, so necessary for opposing 'our old enemies of England'.

There was a vicar who was very keen on his golf. He went into the pulpit one Matins and horrified the congregation with his text. 'What shall it profit a man' he roared fervently, 'if he gain the whole world and lose the last hole?'

The coward's way out

A vicar of Hale St Peter had made a 'pig's ear' of a golf match he was playing in, and at length became well and truly bunkered. He tried almost every club in his bag but the ball was still there. He whispered to his partner, the president of the club,

'What shall I take now?'

His partner, who was one of his faithful parishioners, looked at the ground and said, with a tremble in his voice,

'Poison, Vicar.'

K.Y.B.H.D.

An English archdeacon was spending a holiday in Scotland and fulfilled an ambition of a lifetime by playing a round of golf at St Andrews. Whether it was the excitement of the occasion or just a bad patch, he began badly. He topped his drive, he topped his second, and third shot; finally he turned to his caddie a dour Scot, and said,

'I really must do better than this. Perhaps a little prayer while I'm playing my next shot will help.' With great deliberation he played his fourth shot and topped the ball again.

'I just can't understand it,' exploded the archdeacon, 'and I prayed over it too.'

The caddie came to his rescue: 'When we pray in the Presbyterian Kirk, we always keep our heads down!'

Golf is the pursuit of pale pills by purple people

An old bishop was playing a solid round of golf, but at the tenth hole his ball got badly lodged in a bunker making him blurt out angrily, 'Aswan.'

'Why do you say that?' asked his playing companion.

'Because,' said the bishop with tight lips, 'it's the biggest dam I know.'

Holy innocence

When Archdeacon D.E.M. Glynne-Jones was Vicar of Wrexham he was Captain of the Golf Club for a season. The story went round his staff of curates that one of his lady parishioners had recently become a member and as she was leaving church one evening the Vicar greeted her. 'Ah! Mrs Thomas, I hear you've become a member of the Golf Club. Have you been round yet?'

'Yes, vicar,' came the reply, 'I played last week.'

'What did you go round in?' asked the vicar, attempting to wear two hats in the tone of his voice.

'Oh just the usual you know: skirt and jumper.'

Don't sound the 'l' in golf; speak of it as goff, not gauff (*Etiquette for Men* 1919)

The Vicar of Hale, speaking at a Captain's Dinner at Ringway Golf Club, ventured that the *nouveau riche* moving into an urban area sometimes presented problems at the local Golf Club, especially if they had never played the game before. He implied he was present when one of these quick-rich business men appeared on the course with a caddie to play his first round as a member.

'Do you like a 'igh tee, Sir?' asked the caddie.

'Certainly not!' came the pompous reply, 'we 'ave dinner at eight. Get on with your job and stick the ball on the 'ump.'

The last hole

A bishop and his chaplain had just finished a round of golf and the chaplain as usual had lost.

'Do you know, you'll get your own back one day,' said the bishop to the young chaplain, 'when you bury me.'

'No I won't,' said the keen-witted chaplain, 'it will still be your hole!'

'——GREAT! . . . ALL YOU NEED NOW ARE FIVE LOAVES, AND YOU COULD FEED THE WHOLE VILLAGE.'

12
HOLY HUNT'N, SHOOT'N, AND FISH'N

Thou shalt not

It is recorded that Bishop Blomfield of London used to deliver the following charge to the clergy of his diocese:

'Hunt not, fish not, shoot not,
Dance not, fiddle not, flute not,
Be sure you have nothing to do with Whigs,
But stay at home and feed your pigs;
And above all, I make it my particular desire,
That at least once a week you dine with the squire.'

Orthodoxy is my doxy

The Reverend James Russell, the sporting parson, who was the vicar of Swimbridge, once advertised for a curate as follows:

'Wanted—a curate for Swimbridge; must be a gentleman of moderate and orthodox views.'

Some of the parishioners were puzzled about the meaning of the term 'orthodox' so they consulted the parish clerk.

'Ah,' said the latter, 'I think it means a chap as can ride well to hounds!'

Foxes and Foxtrots

During the last century a curate was taken to task by his diocesan bishop on account of his fondness for the worldly pursuit of fox hunting.

'My Lord,' pleaded the curate, 'fox hunting is no more worldly than dancing, and I understand that your Lordship has been seen at a dance.'

'Now that's true,' replied the bishop, 'but I was never within three rooms of the dance.'

'Quite so, my Lord, quite so,' replied the curate, 'and I was never within three fields of the fox.'

A well-trapped bore

A missionary who had recently returned from a tour in Africa was in a company where there was a man who boasted continually of his great hunting feats, while on safari. After the boaster had monopolized the conversation for a long time, the missionary said,

'I have been in Africa for five years but I haven't done anything to come up to your experiences. There was one occasion though when I did have a nasty time. I was in the bush and I put down my gun under a tree and walked a couple of yards, when all of a sudden a lion ran out of the bush at me.'

'What did you do?' said the hunter, with baited breath.

'Well,' said the missionary, 'I just seized his upper jaw with my right hand and his lower jaw with my left hand and held his mouth open 'till he starved to death.'

No eye for colour

A bishop of the Church of England was staying with with one of his relations, the then Earl of Powis. He was taken out for a day's shooting and was placed in the point of best advantage, with the head keeper. As the birds flew over, the old bishop fired but missed every single one, to the great annoyance of the head gamekeeper. Finally, towards the end of the day, a white pheasant got up, a rare bird in that part of the world, appearing only once every four or five years. The bishop set his gun on it and brought it down at the first shot. Muttered the headkeeper so that everyone could hear, 'If the bishop decides to come next year we will have to paint all the devils white.'

There goes another Feather Failure

The young curate who had become the incumbent at Castle Caereinion in Montgomeryshire, was taken out soon after his arrival by the son of one of the local farmers, and had been introduced to the art of shooting.

'Well,' said the old farmer to his son when he returned from his day's shooting with the parson, 'How did the Rector shape?'

'The young Rector shot sublimely, Father, but God was merciful to the birds.'

Half a den of thieves

The rector of a country parish soon after the pheasant season opened, was making his way to church, when he passed the local gamekeeper. The rector chided him on his neglect to attend the services.

'Well you see, Rector,' said the gamekeeper, 'if I came to church it would result in your congregation becoming smaller, not larger.'

'What do you mean, my man?' asked the rector, thinking the headkeeper was just making excuses.

'Oh it's quite simple,' said the gamekeeper, 'if I came to church half your congregation would take advantage of my being there and would stay away to poach my birds.'

Biblical criticism

A country parson was once going out for a day's shooting dressed in his clerical collar when he met one of the ladies of the village.

'I have never come across any reference to the Apostles having gone shooting,' she snapped.

'That is true,' replied the gun-carrying rector, 'shooting in Palestine was bad; they went fishing instead.'

Fishing aid to evangelism or courting

'You see the ways the fisherman doth take
To catch the fish; what engines doth he make?
Behold! how he engageth all his wits;
Also his snares, lines, angles, hooks and nets;
Yet fish there be, that neither hook nor line,
Nor snare, nor net, nor engine, can make thine:
They must be groped for, and be tickled too,
Or they will not be catch'd, whate'er you do.'

(*John Bunyan*)

The gentle art

One day a stranger wishing to get some fly-fishing said to an old verger, 'Can you tell me if I should have any chance of practising "the gentle art" here?'

'Well, we have a good many pretty and nice ladies in the parish but I can't tell ye what they might say to your honour, on such a point as that; or if so be that their fathers would reckon you a good enough partner for them; but you might try what you can do.'

No so much a misunderstanding more, a way of life

Jimmy maintained in Sunday school that the story he liked best from the Bible was 'the one where everybody loafs and fishes.'

A fisher-man out fished

A parson out fishing one day, came across another angler who was sitting by the side of a dried up pool dangling his line over the mud. The parson, playing the Good Samaritan, went over to him and touched him on the shoulder, and suggested that he might like to come along to the local inn for a drink. Over a pint of bitter the parson, anxious to see whether the man was in his right mind or not, asked the angler if he had caught many that day.

Draining his glass, the other replied blandly, 'Quite a few, you are the twelfth.'

To Banbury came I, O profane one!
Where I saw a Puritane-one
Hanging of his cat on Monday,
For killing of a mouse on Sunday.

A small boy was returning home one Sunday morning after a successful fishing visit to the local river when he ran into the priest coming away from church. In order to avoid the rebuke which was obviously coming his way for breaking the Sabbath the lad held out the fish in front of the priest and said,

'See what these fish have got for nibbling the bait on the Sabbath.'

A turned up nose

A vicar was doing some sea fishing from a pier when a small lad fishing alongside him caught a good sized plaice, which he removed from his hook and threw back into the water.

'Why did you do that?' asked the vicar.

'Well,' came the lad's reply, 'I didn't want one that had been trodden on.'

Two by two

It is thought probable by ancient piscatorial writers that the art of Angling was developed by Noah, since after the deluge, fish were the only creatures not destroyed.

There is the story about the Sunday school teacher who asked her class how Noah might have spent his time while on board the Ark. As there was no reply, she prompted them:

'Do you think he did a lot of fishing?'

'What!' responded an aggressive eight-year-old, 'with only two worms?'

'I'M SORRY, THE VICAR'S JUST GONE OUT—IT'S TIME FOR HIS DAILY ROUND . . .'

13
CONFOUNDED CLERICS

Credibility gap

'What's your new parson like?' asked a visiting layman of the churchwarden of a rural parish.

'Pretty poor,' came the reply, 'we seldom get sight of him. Six days of the week he's invisible, and on the seventh, he's incomprehensible.'

Rotten rhetoric

Said a verger to the incumbent who had remarked that there was dry rot in the church, and especially in the floor:

'Why, bless you sir, the dry rot in the floor is not very much when you compare it to the dry rot in the pulpit, and that's been getting worse ever since you came here!'

Tempora mutantur (the times are changed)

Father Archer of St Peter's, Oughtrington, told the story of a seventy year-old incumbent in a small Cornish parish. He had served his people faithfully for thirty-six years. The bishop of the diocese wrote to him suggesting that he had been in the parish too long and that he should either move, or, preferably, retire. The old rector wrote back to the bishop, saying:

'My Lord, when I was offered this parish by your predecessor but five there was no suggestion given that the post was to be temporary.'

Noxia herba nicoteana

A caller once, when entering Dr Spurgeon's study, found him smoking.

'At your idol again,' he commented.

'Yes,' said the great preacher, 'but as you can see, I am burning it!'

Less room for the lesser prophets

A visiting preacher arrived to officiate one Sunday in a country parish where he was to be accommodated for the night in the vicarage. He was shown to a very small room instead of the usual best bedroom which was normally reserved for visitors.

'Is this the bedroom?' asked the visiting preacher in amazement.

'Aye, sir, this the prophet's chamber.'

'It must be for one of the *minor* prophets then,' was the quick reply.

Aitch ache

In the North of England there was an incumbent who found it almost impossible to sound his aitches and at evening service one Sunday he had the most awful headache. As the lady of the manor came out of church she greeted him, asking kindly of his health.

'I'm not very well, this evening, I've got such a 'orrid 'eadache. Do you know of anything I could take for it?'

'Why not try a couple of apirates Vicar?' she said.

Riddle me riddle me ree

The American bishop, James Pike, once suggested that the Church's mission would be relieved of a heavy piece of luggage if it could get rid of the traditional formulation of the doctrine of the Trinity. He related a story told by Cardinal Cushing of Boston, who, when he was a parish priest, was called to the side of a man who had collapsed in a department store. Cushing had asked the man: 'Do you believe in God the Father, God the Son, and God the Holy Ghost?'

The man opened one eye and said to those around him, 'Here am I dying, and he's asking me riddles!'

Confession on the run

The young lad coming out from Sunday school was running so fast that he tripped over the curate's feet. Picking him up and dusting him down the curate asked,

'Why were you running so fast Raymond?'

'I was trying to stop two lads from scrapping, Father.'

'Which two?' demanded the curate, his well-trained eyes scanning the play ground.

'Please Father,' said Raymond, 'Paul Wakefield over there, and me!'

Self inflicted

A young cleric who was very keen on social work and very good at pastoral visiting had spent a great deal of time in the down-town area of the parish. He spoke endlessly to his vicar about the sufferings of the poor.

'But are you sure they suffer?' asked the vicar.

'Of course I am,' came the reply, 'why, I go into their houses and talk to them for hours on end.'

Enforced rest

Two people were travelling in a railway compartment and the one said to the other,

'Look here, old boy, I met your vicar when I was abroad on holiday. He told me he had come out to Majorca for a rest but he hardly looked as if he needed one.'

'Ah,' said the other feelingly, 'but we did!'

Heresy hunter

A vicar of a North Wales parish who had a large staff of curates noticed that whenever he preached in the parish church one dear stalwart lady, superintendent of the Sunday school, always nodded off to sleep but when one of the curates preached she always remained awake in rapt attention marking every word which was uttered. The vicar took her to task over this and asked for the reason.

'Well, I'll tell you vicar,' she said. 'When you preach I know that the word of God is safe, but when those young fellows have a try it's my duty to make sure that their doctrine is sound.'

Higher purchase

It was the Rev Dr Hunt's great ambition to have a stall in some cathedral, where he might enjoy his favourite music, and he always thought that his friend the Bishop of L—— would gratify his wishes. He even gave his Lordship the following hint. He had procured the bishop some cheeses for which his parish was famous, and on being asked how he should be paid for them, the worthy vicar answered, 'By *instalments*, if your Lordship pleases.' The hint however, was never taken.

A saintly plea

Henry Parry Liddon was appointed to a Canonry at St Paul's on 16 February 1870, but unlike the majority of the superior clergy, he never adopted 'Canon' as a title. To any friends who addressed him as 'Canon Lidon', he would say, 'Please do not Canonize me.'

Dean's thunder plundered

Once, Dean Hole had the misfortune to attend a public meeting where the chairman in his introductory remarks covered the ground that he should have left for the Dean to speak upon. Finally he finished, and said, 'Now the Dean will give his address.'

The Dean rose and said, 'My address is, The Deanery, Rochester, and I am going back there at once.'

Shortest sermon ever

It is said that the shortest sermon ever preached was that of Dean Swift when preaching a charity sermon. He took the text, 'He that hath pity on the poor lendeth unto the Lord, and that which he hath given will be repaid to him again.' The Dean followed this with,

'Now, my friends, you hear the terms of the loan. If you like the security, down with the cash!'

Be not anxious saying, 'what shall we eat?'

Dean Stanley was entertaining two friends to dinner. The duck was cold and the Dean was carving but he became so involved in the conversation that he allowed the duck to slide from the plate onto the floor. One of the guests, who saw that the fare on the dinner table was somewhat sparse, said hurriedly, 'I see a cat in the room; a cat Mr Dean!'

'Don't be alarmed for the duck,' replied the Dean, 'I have my foot on it.'

Stretching it

On February 23 1914, Dean Inge recorded the following anecdote about Dr Jowett of Balliol:

Jowett was asked by a pupil: 'Do you really think, Master, that the stoics or epicureans were right in saying that a good man might be happy on the rack?'

Jowett's reply was superb. 'Well, perhaps a very good man on a very bad rack.'

Blimey

Walking through Christ Church quadrangle one morning at the beginning of term Dean Jackson met some undergraduates who passed him by without doffing their caps. The Dean called after them and asked,

'Do you know who I am?'

'No, sir,' came the reply.

'Well, how long have you been in college?' asked the Dean.

'Eight days, sir,' came the answer.

'Oh! Very well,' said the Dean, walking away with a smile, 'even puppies don't open their eyes until the ninth day.'

Hell is full of good meanings and wishes

The background is the church of St Paul's, Bloor Street, Toronto, about which the Rev. Ted Grey writes: 'The city was quite English in the early days a century ago, then about sixty years later it burgeoned tremendously and built a very big church a couple of miles from "downtown" on Bloor Street East, which specialized in great preachers. One of the first, if not the very first incumbent was Canon Cody, a little man, granite faced, and well-known throughout Toronto.

'He was a visitor at an exclusive golf club and having finished his round one day was sitting Canadian fashion in the locker room, dressed in a towel after his shower and having a drink with his friends. A tycoon passed by and looked hard at him, came back and stared at him again. He said to Cody, "Where in hell have I seen you before?" '

' "I don't know," answered the good Canon, "what part of Hell do you come from?" '

Hell and chancery are always open

Dean Swift was at dinner on one occasion when an ill-mannered young laywer said to him, 'Mr Dean, suppose the parsons and the Devil went to law, which do you think would win the case?'

'Undoubtedly the Devil would,' said Dean Swift, 'for you see all the lawyers would be on his side.'

Fire insurance

Speaking at the annual dinner of a large insurance company, Dean Lefroy was asked by one of the guests, 'Aren't you a bit out of your sphere?'

'Oh not at all,' replied the Dean, 'this Company insures people against one kind of fire, and it is the duty of the clergy to insure them against another type.'

Horse bites—clergyman blamed

The steed bit his master;
  How came this to pass?
He heard the good pastor
  Cry, 'All flesh is grass.'

14
BENCH-BOUND BRETHREN

Semper gaudentes sint ista sede sedentes
(Blessed may they be who occupy this seat)

At one time in history there existed a bitter struggle for precedence between the sees of Canterbury and York. This came to a climax in 1176 when, at a Church Council held in Westminster Abbey, the Archbishop of York coming in and seeing the Papal Legate on a throne, with the Archbishop of Canterbury sitting on his right, 'strove irreverently to sit down between the Legate and his Grace of Canterbury, thrusting with the more uncomely quarters of his body so that he sat down on the lap of his own Primate.'

This lap-sitting incident led to an unseemly brawl when the supporters of each side joined in with staves and fists, and it is said that his Grace of York found himself full length on the floor in grave danger of being hammered to death.

The dispute was referred to the Pope who, with the wisdom of Solomon, decided that 'in future, York should bear the title of *Primate of England*, and Canterbury that of *Primate of All England*,' which titles have continued in use to the present day.

Common Market complication

English episcopal titles have from time to time proved almost too much for the foreigner: a Bishop of Bath and Wells on holiday on the continent had his name entered in the hotel register by the clerk as 'L'Evêque de Bain et Puits'; and a Bishop of Sodor and Man as 'L'Evêque du Siphon et d'Homme'.

In the purple

When Wilberforce was a bishop it was the custom for members of the episcopate to wear dark purple beetle-shell suits at dinners and on formal occasions. He was dressed thus when a person asked him why he wore such a peculiarly coloured evening dress.

He replied, 'Because a bishop must be inviolate!'

Diminutive beasts of burden

Geoffrey Fisher, Bishop of Chester, 1932–1939, was talking on one occasion to a group of Mothers Union members. He was dealing with the theme of worldly goods and possessions.

'My assets,' he said, 'are my sons.' And from that time onwards, his six sons were known in the Diocese of Chester as the 'Bishop's assets'.

Top and tail

It is said that when Archbishop Whately was present at the Privy Council, he used to stand with his back to the fire, his coat tails draped over his arms in order the better to warm his seat, and thus successfully excluding all the heat from the others present.

One man, who used to keep his hat on, gave rise to the Archbishop's remark: 'A bishop keeps uncovered that which ought to be covered, and a peer keeps covered that which ought to be uncovered.'

The morning after

Bishop Stubbs was walking down the street one morning when he met a friend who had sat near him at a banquet on the previous night. The friend enquired anxiously if the bishop had got home all right.

The bishop looked somewhat surprised and then, with his tongue in his cheek replied, 'Oh yes, thank you, it was only my boots that were tight!'

A saint-biting sinner

When Bishop Barnes of Birmingham said that St Francis was dirty, and probably flea-ridden as well, many Roman Catholics were furious and spoke in solemn wrath. Chesterton simply answered with the following biting rhyme:

A Broad-minded Bishop Rebukes the Verminous St Francis

If Brother Francis pardoned Brother Flea,
There still seems need of such strange charity,
Seeing he is, for all his gay good will,
Bitten by funny little creatures still.

No small change

When Archbishop Magee was Bishop of Peterborough, he went on a rest cure. On leaving the hotel he received his bill and was aghast at its amount. He paid it without complaint, however, and gave the waiter a tip.

As he was leaving, the proprietor came to him and said,

'I hope your Lordship has found the rest and change which he needed.'

'Indeed I haven't,' replied Archbishop Magee with feeling, 'the waiter has got the change, you've got the rest, and I've got nothing.'

We must speak by the card, or equivocation will undo us (*Shakespeare: Hamlet*, *V*, *i*)

Mr W. E. Gladstone met Archbishop Magee on one occasion and said to him:

'I understand my Lord that you do not quite approve of my dealing with the Irish Question.'

The Archbishop replied; 'It's not your dealing Mr Gladstone to which I object, it's your shuffling!'

The not-so-dumb ox

When Wilberforce was Bishop of Oxford it was his custom to dine occasionally at an establishment frequented by farmers at Banbury. On one occasion having little appetite, he explained that he was, as it were, 'off his feed.'

'Try Thorley's food, my Lord,' suggested one of the farmers present facetiously, referring to a brand of animal feed-stuffs.

'That,' replied the Bishop, 'is good for horses and I see it is good for asses but it might not suit Oxon!'

A mountainous request

During the reign of George II, there was a certain Rev Dr Mountain who had obtained preferment for himself by his industry and had become Bishop of Durham. When the Archbishopric of York became vacant and the King did not know whom to appoint, he consulted Dr Mountain, who replied;

'Hads't thou faith as a grain of mustard-seed thou wouldest say to this mountain, "Be removed hence and be cast into the *see*!" '

Bishop-maker

It would be a brave Prime Minister now who would appoint a bishop purely for his political affiliation. It was, however, Lord Melbourne, who took a bishop to task for voting against him in the House of Lords. When the bishop replied, 'I owe a duty to my Lord and Maker,' Melbourne retorted, 'You may remember your Lord, but you have forgotten your maker.'

A good bishop

It is said that the reign of a bishop can be divided into three parts. During the first part, when he is made a bishop, he is always afraid that he is doing wrong.

During the second part of his reign he is always sure he is doing right, and, during the third part of his reign, he doesn't care a brass farthing whether he is doing right or wrong; and then he is a good bishop.

'Gone,' blustered the bishop, 'where has he gone? It's his business to be here.'

'Well,' my Lord,' came the reply, 'I wouldn't like to commit myself as to where he's gone but he died this morning.'

False colours

On one occasion a churchwarden complained to Bishop Stubbs of Oxford that the curate of his parish wore a hood very similar to that of an Oxford M.A. which he certainly was not.

'The man has a lie upon his back my Lord,' said the outraged churchwarden.

'Don't say a lie, Mr Churchwarden,' replied Bishop Stubbs, 'say a false-hood.'

Pauline approval

Canon Parkinson was very highly thought of by the working classes in Manchester and was once attacked by a lay-opponent on the large salaries paid to bishops.

'What, sir,' demanded his protagonist, 'would the Apostle Paul have said could he have seen the present day life of luxury led by our prelates and church dignitaries as they roll around in their carriages and live in their palaces?'

'Well,' said the Canon, pretending to think very deeply about the question, 'I think he would have said, "Hello, things in the Church are looking up".'

SUBJECT INDEX